DISCOVERING
MACHINE KNITTING

From deciphering the machine to designing your own

Kandy Diamond

DISCOVERING
MACHINE KNITTING

From deciphering the machine to designing your own

THE CROWOOD PRESS

CONTENTS

~~~~~~~~~~~~~~~~~~~~

INTRODUCTION

Welcome to the world of machine knitting! I have been machine knitting since 2002 and am here to help you discover this wonderful craft. The picture shows me in my studio working at my knitting machine; this is the kind of machine I will be teaching you to get to grips with throughout the book. Covering everything from troubleshooting and looking after the machine to using more advanced techniques such as intarsia and shaping, I am here to help you fall in love with your knitting machine.

The purpose of this book is to help demystify machine knitting, starting from first principles with how the machine works and how stitches are formed, through to shaping garment panels to your desired size and fit. The book aims to help you gain confidence in machine knitting so you can enjoy working with your machine. If you work through the step-by-step instructions and projects in this book, by the end of it you will be designing and knitting your own garments.

This isn't just about teaching you how to use a knitting machine, though – it is also about celebrating the huge potential for creative design and making in machine knitting. For a book that is suitable for beginners, I have covered a huge range of techniques, so whether you love to knit stripes or want to get creative with punch cards, there is something in here for you.

This is my studio space, where I design and make all my knits. The Brother KH881 domestic knitting machine was used throughout this book.

This selection of knitted swatches shows the variety of fabrics you can create using a domestic knitting machine.

This book focuses on using a standard-gauge domestic knitting machine; I have used a second-hand Brother model, but all of the information applies to any domestic knitting machine – just use your manual to find the relevant switch/function on your machine. Step-by-step instructions are accompanied by clear photographs to show you exactly what needs to happen at each stage of any new process.

With all the instructions, I have avoided using abbreviations and have aimed to explain things as I would if I were talking you through the process. I find abbreviations and specialist terminology can be off-putting, making machine knitting patterns and instructions inaccessible for beginners; I wanted instead to provide instructions that are user-friendly and straightforward.

I have structured the book so that you can work your way through it in order, developing your skills as you go. Each chapter focuses on a specific area of knit design, such as shaping or creating patterned knits, with step-by-step instructions for each technique. Chapters 2 to 7 all end with a project, so that you can apply the skills you have learned to creating a finished piece.

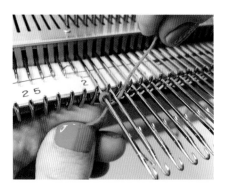

Photographs such as these are used throughout the book to help communicate techniques and processes.

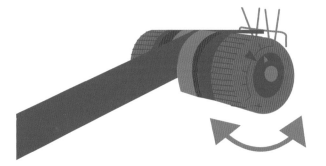

Some things are clearer in diagram form.

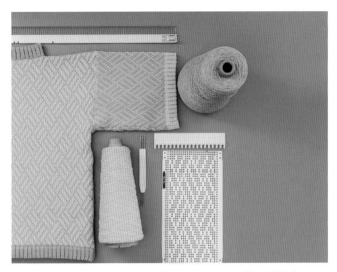

Chapter 3 covers how to knit a simple top using a punch card for the fabric patterning.

As well as teaching skills and techniques, I wanted to provide context and inspiration for your machine knitting. With this in mind, I have included designer profiles of a variety of machine knitters who use this craft to create a broad range of interesting knits. I hope that these profiles will help demonstrate the huge range of pieces that can be created with a knitting machine, as well as giving you an insight into their practice.

From taking you on a tour around the machine and teaching you how it works, to going through techniques and projects, this book is very hands-on, so let's take it to your knitting machine and get stuck in!

This is one of the featured designers, Shelby Marie Fuller, and an example of her work.

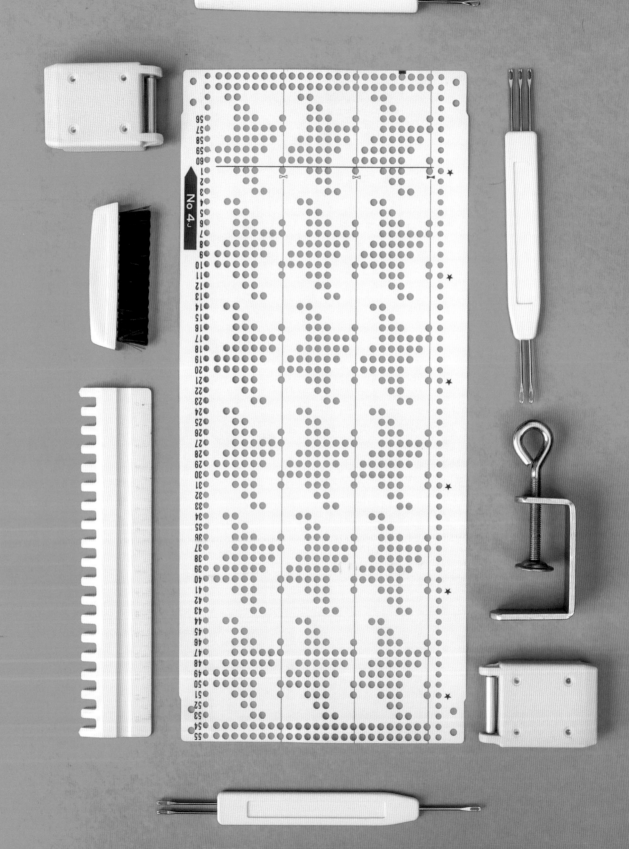

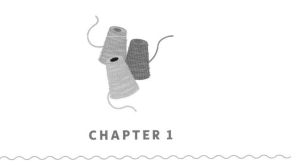

CHAPTER 1

BEFORE YOU START

There are a few things that are useful to know before you begin using your knitting machine. This chapter will help you to find your way around the machine and give you some useful information on how it works, how to look after it and what kinds of yarns are most suitable. This chapter may look like quite dense, but is packed with information that will help you get on with and understand your machine.

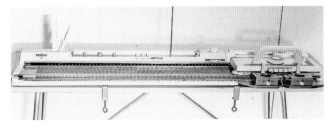

Domestic knitting machine with punch-card function.

THE KNITTING MACHINE

Whether you are looking to buy a knitting machine or already own one, you have probably realised that there are many different makes and models to choose from. One of the most affordable ways to get one is to select from the wide variety that is available second-hand. These range from a simple plastic Bond machine with no yarn feeder to Brother electronic machines with programming capabilities, and the selection can be quite overwhelming. So how do you know what's right for you? Well, that depends on what you want to create.

For plain or striped knits, any standard domestic knitting machine will work for you; a chunky machine is also an option if you are interested in working with thicker yarns. If you want some patterning in your designs, go for a knitting machine with a punch-card function. The patterns you create using a punch-card machine will always be repeating designs.

For larger placement motifs or graphic patterns that you can program the machine to knit, you would want an electronic machine, which gives you broader patterning capabilities and is usually used along with a computer and software to create your designs. These are then downloaded to the machine rather than being input using a punch card.

If you want to be able to create true, stretchy ribs you will need a ribber bed; these can be bought separately and added to most single-bed domestic knitting machines.

Although these machines can look quite different and have varying capabilities, the basics of how the machine knits are the same. This process involves a needle bed, needles, a carriage, and, of course, the all-important yarn! It's time to look at a knitting machine and explain what I'm talking about.

GETTING TO KNOW YOUR KNITTING MACHINE

Your knitting machine might look a bit different to the one I'm using in this book, but the main parts will be the same, so that's where we're starting.

We will go into detail about different parts and functions when we get to using them, but for now we will tackle the basics, starting with the needle bed.

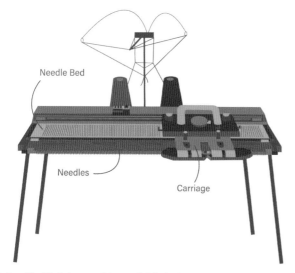

A simplified knitting machine, with labels showing the three parts that we will be looking at first.

Needle Bed

Every knitting machine will have a needle bed – the large, flat part of the machine where all the needles sit. As shown in the photograph, there are slots in the top of the machine – one slot for each needle – equally spaced so the gap between the needles is completely even, which will make your knitted stitches evenly spaced.

The needle bed will also be marked, usually at the end, with letters or numbers, representing different needle positions. Mine is labelled with the letters A, B, D and E. Have a look at these markings and check your machine manual to see what the different positions are.

You might see the term 'gauge' used when referring to knitting machines. With industrial machines, the gauge is calculated by the number of knitting needles in an inch on the machine, so a 10-gauge machine would be used for knitting fine fabrics and a 2.5-gauge for a chunky fabric. Domestic knitting machines come with fine, standard or chunky gauges, which are nice and self-explanatory; these machines have different-sized needles and require different tools and accessories. The knitting machine used throughout this book is a standard-gauge domestic machine.

The Needles

In the needle bed are the needles, which have specific parts that work along with the carriage and yarn to create knitted stitches. In a domestic knitting machine, these are called latch needles, and, if you look closely at them, you'll see each needle has a small latch that opens and closes.

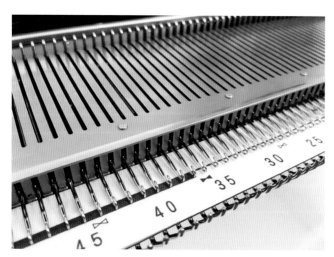

The needle bed is the biggest part of the knitting machine.

Needle position markings help you set needles in the right place.

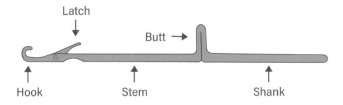

The latch needle and its parts.

As well as the latch, each needle has some other distinctive features that are important for us to understand. The hook at the end of the needle is the part that catches the yarn; this works along with the latch and the movement made by passing the carriage across the needle bed to create new stitches. Another important part of the latch needle is the butt, which is the part that sticks out from the needle bed; this is the bit that makes contact with the carriage when it is moved across the needle bed.

The Carriage

This is where things will start looking different between models; although the functions that the carriage performs will be very similar on most machines, in appearance it's the part that varies the most. This variety is purely a matter of design: different makes of machine will place and label their dials and switches in different ways. For now, we are looking at the most basic function of the carriage and that is to move the needles up and down.

To help you understand the relationship between your carriage and the needles, remove your sinker plate (if you have one) and put a section of needles into working position. Now very slowly move the carriage across the needle bed and watch the needles move up and back down again. What you are seeing as you do this is the needles being forced to move by the track inside the carriage.

Now slide your carriage all the way off the machine, and have a look underneath it at the bit that was touching the needle bed. This will vary slightly between machines, but there will always be at least one track for the needles to move through, and the shape of this track forces the needles to move up and down. This movement of the needles combined with yarn is what creates the knitted stitches.

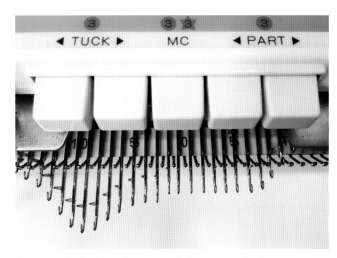

Carriage with the sinker plate removed, showing needles in various positions.

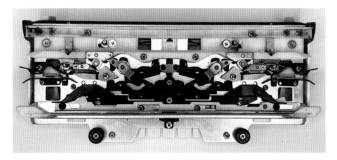

The inside of a knitting machine carriage, showing the tracks that the needle butts move along.

How Stitches are Formed

When using a knitting machine, the latch needle, yarn and carriage movement come together to form stitches. The illustrations overleaf show the steps of stitch formation; as you can see, the opening and closing of the latch is key. This is why it's important that all your machine needles are in good condition; a bent latch or hook can cause problems with stitches not forming, yarn building up and so on.

The illustration just shows what one needle is doing, but the beauty of a knitting machine is that however many needles you have in working position, they will all be doing the same, just at slightly different times. And because they are all right next to each other, the stitches are linked together and every pass of the carriage creates a new row of knitted stitches.

Needle is moving up towards you and the stitch is travelling down the needle

Latch has been forced open by the stitch moving down the needle

Yarn is laid into the hook of the needle as the carriage is passed over the needle

Needle moves down, previous stitch forces the latch to close as it moves back up the needle.

Needle continues to move down, new yarn is pulled through previous loop to form a new stitch.

TOOLS AND ACCESSORIES

All knitting machines will come with some tools and accessories; these might vary slightly between machines, but, typically, you will get the following:

Brush A small brush is handy for cleaning your machine.

Clamps These are used to secure the knitting machine to the table or surface you are using it on.

Claw weights These weights are hung onto the comb or directly onto the knitted fabric to give the fabric some take-down tension and help it knit smoothly.

Comb This is used to hang weights from when casting on; combs come in different lengths.

Latch tool This tool provides you with the end of a latch needle on a tool; it can be used for casting off, picking up dropped stitches and reworking stitches.

Needle pusher This is used to push a number of needles up at the same time; the edge that has spaces in it is used when you want to select just some of the needles.

Ravel cord This shiny, smooth piece of yarn can be used to cast on with, or to separate main knitting and waste yarn.

Transfer tools These are used to transfer stitches and come with different numbers of prongs; multiple prongs allow you to transfer multiple stitches at the same time.

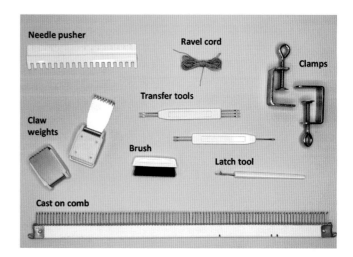

LOOKING AFTER YOUR KNITTING MACHINE

With a huge number of knitting machines being bought second-hand, we know that these machines are built to last, but they're not indestructible. As with any machine, knitting machines behave best when they are well looked after, so here are some general maintenance tips worth following.

Cover it up!

When you're not using the machine, simply covering it with a cloth can save extra cleaning. Some machines come with a plastic cover, and you can also buy plastic covers for knitting machines. Plastic is used because it will keep all the dust off and doesn't have fibres like a cloth does, but you don't need a fancy cover – a thick piece of fabric either draped over the machine or sewn to a shape that fits around it will work.

A simple cover can save a lot of unnecessary cleaning.

Removing fluff from a knitting machine helps to prevent build-up of fibres in the carriage.

Get Rid of That Fluff

Every time you use the machine, fibres from the yarn you are using are deposited on it. The amount of fibres will vary depending on the yarns used, but it's good practice to brush any fibres off the machine between knits.

Most machines come with a small brush to do this, and that works, but I find a 1.5cm-wide (half-inch) paintbrush is quicker and more effective for the surface of the machine. This regular de-fluffing can help to prevent both fuzzy build-up inside the carriage and bits of fluff from getting in your knitting.

Carriage Cleaning

If your knitting goes smoothly and you don't take your carriage off very much, it can be really easy to miss all the fluff and dirt that can build up inside it. Depending on the make/model of the machine, the inside of the carriage will look different and need a slightly different method of cleaning.

On all carriages, focus on removing any fluff using a brush. If there are areas you can't reach with a brush, cotton buds are good; also, compressed air can be great to blast out any fluff or dirt. Run a clean, dry cotton bud along the track inside the carriage to extract any dirt that might have built up in there.

On electronic carriages, pay particular attention to the area where the sensor is located. Wipe the surface and surrounding area of the sensor with a cotton bud to remove any dirt from here.

Cleaning the inside of a knitting-machine carriage can help the machine run smoothly.

This is the oil that I like to use on my knitting machine.

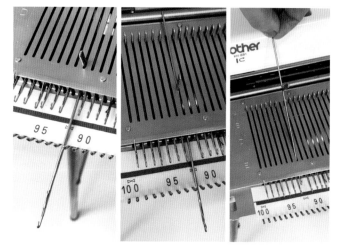

To remove the sponge bar, push it in at one end until the other end sticks out of the machine, then pull the bar out all the way from the end that is sticking out.

Get Oiled

One of the most common mistakes people make when they get a second-hand machine that isn't working properly is to throw oil at it. Old machines often do need oiling but usually not as much as people think, and ideally not with the oil that's been in that machine toolbox for thirty years!

The best oil I have found is called Balistol; specifically made for using on metal components, it is a light oil that works really well on the carriage and needles. I only oil things if they sound or feel creaky or stiff, or when I do a deep clean; over-oiling could result in fluff sticking to the oil inside the carriage, creating a build-up of gunk, which isn't great for all the intricate moving parts of a knitting-machine carriage.

To remove a needle, slide it towards you, push the hook down to force the other end up, then pull the needle up out of the groove by its end.

Deep Clean

Every so often, you need to treat your machine to a deep clean, which is like a spa day for the knitting machine; how often you need to do it will depend on how much you use the machine. A deep clean is exactly what it sounds like. Below are some pointers on the main steps (in order).

Removing and Cleaning Needles

To remove the needles you will take out the sponge bar (or equivalent on your machine) and remove all the needles from the machine. You will usually have a section on the machine that you use the most, so this can be an opportunity to swap the needles from this area with needles from areas you use less.

To clean the needles I use surgical spirit; outdoors if possible, but if not outside, then in a very well-ventilated area. Fill a jar (big enough to hold a group of your needles) half full with spirit and add your needles to it, butts down.

Put the lid on and leave to soak for an hour or so, shaking the container a few times to help release the dirt. Lay some kitchen towel out on a flat surface then, wearing gloves, remove the needles one by one from the jar, wipe to remove any excess dirt and drop a small amount of oil onto the head of the needle where the latch meets the main body of the needle. Place needles on the kitchen towel to allow the spirit to evaporate.

Cleaning the Needle Bed

This part can be tricky, especially with standard domestic machines, as you can't get into the needle spaces to clean them. Compressed air can be really useful for this – use it to blast any fluff out of the needle bed. If there is any dirt build-up on the needle-bed surface, you can use a small amount of surgical spirit on a cloth to wipe this off.

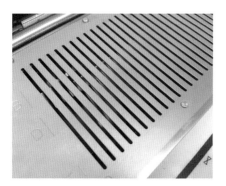

The empty needle bed with all needles removed.

Cleaning inside the carriage using a cotton bud to get into all the channels.

Carriage Deep Clean

This is simply a more involved version of standard carriage cleaning. For the deep clean, use a cotton bud with surgical spirit to clean the channels inside the carriage and remove any build-up of dirt. A small amount of oil can be added to any hinges or areas that move within the carriage; again, use a cotton bud for this to avoid over-oiling.

Put it All Back Together

When everything is clean and the needles are completely dried out, you need to replace the needles. When they are all in, don't forget to put the sponge bar, or your machine's equivalent needle retainer, back in on top of the machine needles. You will need to hold the needles down while sliding the sponge bar back in. You can then put your carriage and sinker plate back on and you're ready to go.

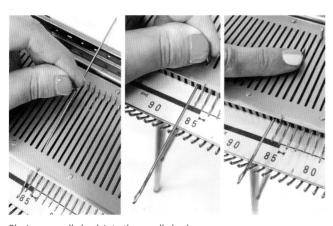

Placing a needle back into the needle bed.

Replacing the sponge bar. Make sure you hold the needles down as you slide it back in.

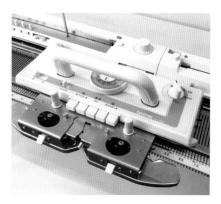

Machine cleaned and ready to knit.

TROUBLESHOOTING

We have looked at the knitting machine and how it functions; now it's time to have a look at what to do if things go wrong, which they sometimes do! You can come back to this section as and when you need it, but if you read through it first, it might help prevent the problems before they occur.

Remember, it is a machine, and as with any machine, the more practice you have at using it, the easier it will become. As with any equipment, there are some common problems, so these are a good place to start.

Carriage Jamming

This is one of the most common problems with machine knitting and can be caused by a number of things. If the carriage does jam, don't panic, and above all don't force it! Forcing can cause needles to bend or break.

Find the carriage-release function on your machine. Moving this lever or switch will disengage your carriage from the needle bed, allowing you to lift the carriage off the machine.

Sometimes, if the carriage is very stuck and won't lift off, you might need to take the metal yarn-feeder section (sinker plate) off, as the needles sometimes get wedged in there. To do this, simply unscrew it carefully then remove it from the carriage and from any needles that it's caught on.

When you have taken the carriage off, take a look at the machine so you can figure out why it got stuck. The most common causes of carriages jamming are the yarn being too thick to go through the machine needles, the yarn being caught under the carriage or sinker plate, or needle/s caught in the sinker plate.

Yarn can easily get caught in the wheels on the sinker plate, which can stop them from moving freely, making the carriage stiff and more difficult to move. If your carriage does get jammed, it is worth checking there isn't a build-up of yarn around these wheels.

Always check all the needles and knitting before replacing the carriage, pick up any dropped stitches and fix or replace any bent/broken needles, and remember to secure the carriage back to the needle bed before resuming your knitting.

Yarn not Knitting

Sometimes when you're knitting, the yarn doesn't catch onto all the needles. This can happen for a few reasons. Stitch size is a common cause, especially if you're changing between yarns; if your stitch size/tension is too small, the stitches won't form because they will be too small to pass over the hook of the needles. If this happens, you need to increase the stitch size so that more yarn is being delivered to the needles and proper stitches can be formed.

Another cause of the yarn not knitting could be that it is caught somewhere, so is not meeting the needles when it passes over. It can get caught up in the sinker plate, gate pegs, or anywhere else it can find to get snagged. This usually happens if the yarn doesn't have enough tension on it, so is often an issue when changing colours because the yarn is slack. If this is the case, you either need to increase the tension on the mast or pull some yarn back towards the cone.

The carriage is stuck over the knitting area.

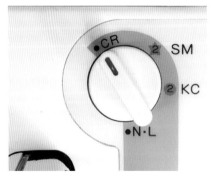
Carriage-release function on the Brother machine.

The carriage being lifted off the machine.

The knitting is too tight, causing the yarn to float over the needles and not knit.

This yarn doesn't have enough tension; this is referred to as slack yarn.

Pulling the yarn back towards the cone to remove the slack.

Loops at the Edge of Knitting

Sometimes you might find small loops forming at the edge of your knitting. This will happen when there is not enough tension on the yarn, and can have a number of different causes:

Taking the carriage too far past the edge of the knitting area
This is a common mistake, especially when working over a small area of needles on your machine. You only need to move the carriage far enough to knit and clear the edge stitches at each side of your knitting.

Not enough input tension on the yarn
Check the dial where the yarn has been brought through on the mast, and increase the tension here if needed.

Slack yarn due to yarn being pulled/moved around between being used
This is common when knitting stripes and swapping between colours, and resting the yarn rather than cutting it. If this happens, pull the yarn back towards the cone to put the tension back into it.

Stitches Falling at the Edge of Knitting

This usually happens when you have taken the carriage too far past the edge of your knitting. When you knit a row, the carriage needs to go past the edge of the knitting but only just past – you don't need to take it all the way to the end of the needle bed. Taking it too far causes slack in the yarn, which in turn means the very edge stitch/es don't knit.

Stitches falling off at the edges can also happen when you are knitting punch-card patterns and can simply be due to the needle arrangement in the pattern you are knitting. If that's the case, you have to keep an eye on the stitches and pick them up if they drop.

Sometimes this can also happen because you're knitting too fast! When everything is set right and the machine is running smoothly, it can be really tempting to speed up, but remember how many things the machine is doing and how much faster it already is than hand knitting, and take it a bit slower.

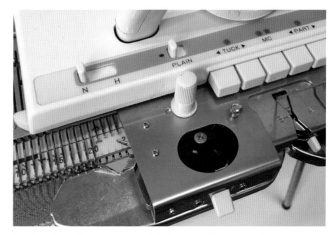

This is as far as the carriage needs to travel past the edge of the knitting area.

Dropped Stitch

Sometimes a stitch will drop off the needle and cause a small ladder in the fabric; this can happen at the edges, but these don't usually ladder and you can pick the stitch up and put it straight onto the edge needle. Dropped stitches often happen when you are transferring, or sometimes if one of the needles isn't working correctly.

If you drop a stitch, the first thing to do is remove your weights, as this will help to prevent it dropping any further down your fabric. When you have done this, take your latch tool, find the dropped stitch and use the latch tool to knit the stitch, closing the ladder. The photos give a step-by-step guide.

This stitch has dropped, and a small ladder has been made in the fabric.

Picking up a Dropped Stitch

1. To pick up a dropped stitch, start by using the hook of the latch tool to find the stitch. Insert the hook into the stitch with the hook facing you.

2. Push the tool down so that the stitch travels up the latch tool. Keep moving the tool down until the stitch moves past the open latch.

3. Now use the ladder to knit the stitch. Start by placing the lowest ladder in front of the latch on your tool.

4. With the stitch behind the latch and the ladder on top of it, pull the tool up: this will pull the ladder through the stitch, forming a new stitch.

5. Repeat steps 2–4 over the remaining ladders, pushing the tool down, placing the ladder in the hook, and pulling the ladder through the stitch on the needle.

6. When you have knitted the top ladder, place the stitch back onto the empty needle on the machine.

Stitch not Forming Correctly

Occasionally a single needle won't work properly, and you will get a faulty stitch in this area. Needles can get bent out of shape and they can even snap. Diagrams and photos earlier in this chapter showed what the latch needle should look like.

The latch needs to be in line with the hook so it can close and the stitch can form properly. Have a good look at the needle; sometimes the latch has simply become a bit wonky and you can straighten it with some pliers. If the needle latch or hook is too damaged to be bent back into shape, however, you will need to replace the needle that isn't working correctly.

This needle has a bent latch, which means that it won't be able to form stitches correctly.

Replacing a Needle

To replace a needle, first you need to remove the sponge bar, as this is holding all the needles in place (*see* the section on deep-cleaning your machine earlier in the chapter). Simply remove the broken needle and replace it with a spare if you have one, or a needle from the very edge of the needle bed. When your new needle/s are in, don't forget to replace the sponge bar. Simply push it back in from one end while holding the needles down with the other hand.

Remember, if the needle isn't knitting correctly, you can often bend the latch and hook back into the right position using small pliers; try this first before replacing the needle with a new one.

YARNS

When you are working with a knitting machine, the yarn that you choose to use can make a huge difference, not only to the fabric you make but also to the physical effort of knitting with it. When choosing which yarns you want to work with, there are obvious qualities such as colour and surface that you will look at, but it's good to also understand what you are working with.

There are so many different yarns to choose from, so understanding a bit more about where these yarns come from and how they are made means you can make more informed choices about what you are using.

Fibres

The yarn you are using will be made from fibres: natural, man-made or a combination of both. Natural fibres include wool, cotton and linen – essentially any fibres that are derived from animals or plants – while fibres such as acrylics, viscose and polyester are all man-made. A common misconception is that all natural fibres are environmentally friendly, and all man-made fibres are not. This is not always the case, as there's much more to a yarn than simply the source of the fibre. There are ethical considerations relating to fibres, such as wool, that come from the fleece of animals, and environmental considerations for resource- and process-intensive fibres, such as cotton.

Whichever yarn you choose, it's important to know that a fabric knitted using a cotton yarn will have a different finish and handle to the same fabric knitted using a wool yarn. Every fibre has its own unique set of characteristics that directly affect the properties of the yarn and, in turn, the fabric it is made into.

So, what does all this mean for you as a machine knitter? Depending on the fibres that the yarn is made from, the yarn will behave differently when being knitted due to the properties of the fibres.

A variety of wool yarns of different qualities and thicknesses.

A selection of cotton machine-knitting yarns.

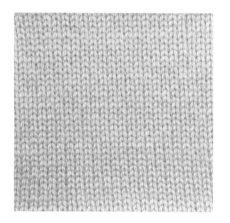

Two ends of fine lambswool yarn knitted into a swatch.

Cotton yarn knitted into a swatch.

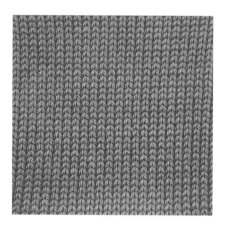

Wool

There are a variety of fibres that are classified as wools, from goat hair to yak and alpaca to camel. However, in machine-knitting yarns, this fibre primarily comes from sheep, and still has many variants. You will come across plenty of lambswool and merino wool, as well as wool and wool/acrylic blends.

Wool fibre has great natural elasticity, meaning good stretch and recovery when being knitted and in the resulting fabric. The unique structure of the wool fibre means that it acts as an insulator in cold weather, but can also draw moisture away from the body. Wool is a naturally renewable and biodegradable fibre that breaks down easily and quickly when buried.

Cotton

This is another very widely used fibre, and again a natural fibre, derived from the boll that grows right at the top of the cotton plant. It is a very water-intensive crop that grows most successfully in hot climates.

Cotton fibres are known for their strength and durability, which in turn make cotton yarns strong and durable. Due to the structure of the fibres, cotton yarns have a low stretch and recovery, meaning that when you knit with them, they might feel stiffer than a wool or acrylic. The fibre has a very smooth surface, which makes it very comfortable when worn against the skin.

Cotton is a natural fibre; however, a huge number of insecticides and pesticides are used in the farming process that can cause harm to both the farmers and surrounding area. Many more organic cottons are now being produced, which have a lower environmental impact.

Acrylic machine-knitting yarns in a few different thicknesses.

A selection of fancy yarns.

Acrylic yarn knitted into a swatch.

Textured fancy 'eyelash' yarn knitted into a swatch.

Acrylic

This yarn is very widely used in knitwear in general, and you will find a lot of acrylic machine-knitting yarns. Acrylic is a man-made yarn made from synthetic polymers that was developed to mimic the properties of wool. It is a versatile fibre, as it can be processed in many different ways to create different types of yarn.

Being modelled on wool, acrylic fibres have good stretch and recovery, and the resultant yarns are often stronger than their woollen counterpart. Acrylic yarns can be great for beginner machine knitters and for people who don't want to wear or use animal fibres. Acrylic is derived from petroleum products such as crude oil; it resists degradation, meaning it will last well while being used, but unfortunately won't biodegrade.

Fancy Yarns

Any yarn that isn't a standard plied and spun yarn can be categorised as 'fancy'. This handy catch-all term for any non-standard yarn covers a huge range of yarns that all have their own specific properties. Some fancy yarns, such as fine 'eyelash' and boucle yarns, will add texture to your knitting, whereas lurex can add shine. You can also find glow-in-the-dark, neon and light-reflective yarns if you want something really out of the ordinary.

Waste Yarn

This refers to a yarn that is knitted at the beginning or end of a swatch or panel that will later be removed. Waste yarn can be used to cast on, particularly to knit lifted hems; it is also used to remove fabric from the machine, leaving you with live stitches at the top of your knitted fabric.

Waste yarn can be any yarn; I usually use a thinner yarn than I am working with for the main knitting, and often an acrylic because it has good strength and flexibility. Despite its name, I try not to waste this yarn by avoiding cutting it where possible (usually when it is used to cast on) and instead winding it back onto the cone after unravelling it from the knitted piece. If it has been cut, it can be tied and wound back onto the cone by hand; using a thin yarn means that any small knots will knit through without causing any problems.

Suitable cotton yarn in the hook of a standard-gauge needle.

Unsuitable yarn in the hook of a standard-gauge needle.

Thickness

One of the most common questions I get asked by beginner machine knitters is 'what yarn should I use?' People often come to machine knitting from hand knitting and want to use the same yarns, and while some hand-knit yarns will work on a standard-gauge knitting machine, there is a whole world of yarns out there that have been made specifically to use with a knitting machine.

To start with, we have to consider different knitting machines; all the projects in this book will be made using a standard-gauge domestic knitting machine, as that is the machine beginners are most likely to have gone for, but there are other machines out there. Within the world of domestic machine knitting, we also have 'chunky' machines and 'fine' machines, for which you would use thicker or thinner yarns respectively.

When choosing a yarn to use on your knitting machine, you want to avoid any yarn that is too thick for the machine because it will not knit, and can cause the machine to jam. You can use thinner yarns, and some great effects can be created by using multiple ends of finer yarns together. A good way to test if a yarn will work with a machine is simply to place the yarn into the hook of one of the needles. There needs to be some room left in the hook of the needle for the yarn to knit, so if the yarn fills the hook up, it will be too thick for the machine. As you can see in the photographs, the finer cotton yarn leaves plenty of room, whereas the chunky cotton fills the hook completely.

In addition to thickness, remember the other properties yarns have that will also affect their suitability for the machine. For example, you would be able to knit with a thicker acrylic yarn than cotton yarn, as the acrylic's greater elasticity enables it to move more easily through the needles.

The yarn examples listed here are all suitable for standard-gauge machines, and the chart provides information relating to the stitch size they have been knitted with.

Yarn type	Ply (count)	Stitch size	Yarn knitted into swatch
Acrylic	Fine 2 ply (2/30s)	0	
Cotton	2 ply	2	
Lambswool	2 ply (2/17s)	2 ⅓	
Wool	2 ply (2/15s)	3	
Acrylic	2 ply (2/10s)	4	
Merino	4 ply	4	
Shetland wool	2 ply (2/10s)	4 ⅔	
Soft cotton	4 ply	5–6	
Mohair/nylon	N/A – Fancy	8–9	

Ria Burns – Ria Burns Knitwear

Ria in her studio.

Yarns and plants used for natural dying.

I'm Ria Burns of Ria Burns Knitwear, based in Bristol, southwest England. I've been machine knitting since 2014 and now run my knitwear label full time. Sustainability, transparency and localism in fashion are incredibly important to me, so my knitwear is made using traceable wool from a local farm, which I dye using plants grown in my back garden.

What brought you to machine knitting and where and how did you learn?

I studied fashion design for my degree, as I loved making clothes, and kept my passion for hand knitting as a hobby. About halfway through the course, I realised knitwear was the direction I wanted to go in. After discussing this with my tutor, I was made aware of knitting machines! I booked onto a workshop at Texere Yarns (now Airedale Yarns) and bought a second-hand Knitmaster, and made my final collection into a knitwear collection! As my uni didn't have a textile department, I am mostly self-taught, although I did attend the three-week Fashion Knitwear Summer School at Nottingham Trent in between second and third year.

Can you tell us about the knitting machines you use now and why they are the right machines for your practice?

I mainly use a Brother KH836 with KR850 ribber. The yarn I use is a gauge that suits these domestic machines, and I like to use punch cards, particularly for Fair Isle patterns. A lot of my knitted accessories are ribbed, so my ribber is always set up with the main machine.

How about your design process – what inspires you?

I like the contrast between man-made and natural. I'm inspired by brutalist architecture, bright yellow lichens and rugged rock strata. I'm always taking photos, which I use as the basis for sketches, which I simplify and abstract. My own dye garden and plants within it inspire me too, as they provide me with the colour for that season.

When you've got your inspiration, how do you take it from idea to the finished product?

I use my abstracted sketches to form the basis of stitch patterns for punch cards. I then look through my natural dye records to start planning the colours, as this can vary depending on how well a certain plant has grown each year. I then develop a palette that forms the basis for accessories and garments. My garment shapes are quite classic and simple, as I want the naturally dyed colour and knitted pattern to be the main focus of my pieces.

Yarns drying after being dyed.

Knitted top created using modular knitting.

This chapter has been all about getting familiar with the knitting machine and yarns before starting to use the machine. Can you tell us about the yarns you use in your work and why it is important to you to work in this way?
All of my knitwear is produced in a bespoke yarn from a farm on the Bristol/Somerset border (about thirty minutes from my studio). As I researched British wool during a Masters study, I found there were very few traceable yarns that were suitable for machine knitting. So I commissioned my own, using Shetland-Romney lambswool from the farm. It is woollen spun to a specification of 2/9nm and comes to me oiled on cones in a natural white and grey.

Any hints and tips on sourcing yarns, in particular for people who are interested in having a more sustainable approach to their making?
My top tip for sourcing is to ask the yarn company or mill if they know where the fibre has come from, and how the yarn is made. If they can trace the yarn back to the original fibre source, they will be happy and proud to tell you how the yarn is made!
Example questions to ask: Do you use traceable wool? Is the wool

shipped via air or water? What dyes are used, and are they GOTS (Global Organic Textile Standard) certified? How do they dispose of their waste water?

Do you have any advice for people who are learning to use a knitting machine? Is there anything you wish you had known when you were starting out?
Always make notes when you are experimenting – the swatch you made without notes is often the one you want to knit a final piece from. I also wish I'd known how important finishing (washing/steaming) your swatches was when I started out, as it makes such a difference to your gauge!

Where can people find your work?
🌐 Riaburns.co.uk
📷 Instagram.com/riaburnsknit

CHAPTER 2

GETTING STARTED

In this chapter we are looking at how to use a knitting machine, from threading up to changing colours and casting off. With machine knitting, threading up correctly and knitting at the right tension for your yarn can make the difference between the machine happily knitting fabric and it simply not working. If you are an absolute beginner, I would suggest that you work your way through the chapter and have a go at all the techniques.

THREADING THE MACHINE

It's time to get started: you've chosen your yarn so now you need to get the machine threaded up. The threading will be slightly different for every machine, but most machines have a mast with specific parts that the yarn has to go through. Instructions on how to do this will be in your machine manual, so I'm just going to go through some tips and important points for this part of the process.

Threading the yarn correctly is really important, as it both guides and, in most cases, puts some tension on the yarn you are using. If you miss one of the places the yarn needs to travel through or don't have enough tension on the yarn, this can cause problems when knitting. Remember to check and change the input tension using the dial depending on the yarn you are using.

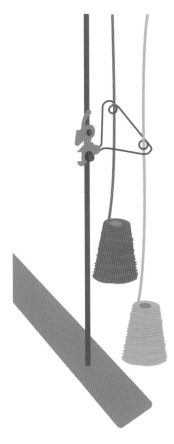

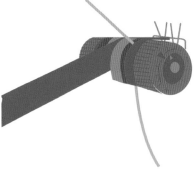

2. The yarn now goes through the hole on the metal guide attached to the mast, straight up, then forward between the tensioning discs. You need to make sure the yarn is travelling between the discs and under the pin.

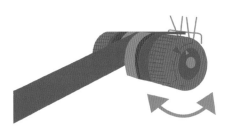

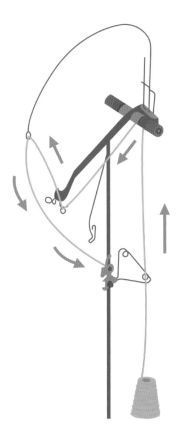

1. Threading the machine. Start by placing the yarn directly underneath the first guide; this can sit either on the table or on the floor. Smaller cones will happily sit on the table, but larger cones might need a bit more room to reel off and be happier on the floor.

3. The dial on the side of the tensioner allows you to reduce or increase the tension on the yarn, depending on the thickness of the yarn: the thinner the yarn, the more tension you want.

4. When you're happy with the tension, take the yarn forward through the next guide, then up through the take-up springs (which resemble antennae) and down through any additional guides, then slide it under the clip on the mast to keep it in place. Now you're ready to look at casting on.

CASTING ON

There are a number of different ways to cast on; choose which one you want to use depending on the kind of finish you want the bottom edge of your fabric to have. You will probably find that you have a preferred method for casting on, but I would recommend you have a go at all the different ways to see how the edge comes out, and keep a sample of each for reference.

To knit a sample, choose a yarn that is smooth and easy to work with. Thread your machine, place the yarn in your carriage's yarn feeder and secure it by tying to a clasp or leg of the machine table. When you have done the cast-on, knit however many rows you want for that swatch, then simply take the yarn out of the carriage and knit across without any yarn to remove the fabric from the machine. This will leave you with an open edge at the top; we will look at how to cast off to make a closed edge later in this chapter.

For now, we are just going to look at casting on onto a single bed; casting on with the ribber will be covered in Chapter 6.

Quick Cast-on with Comb

This cast-on method will give you an open edge. It is good for initial sampling or testing yarn, as it is quick and easy.

1. To cast on with a comb, start by selecting the knitting width on your machine, remembering to centre over the zero. Push all needles you want to knit on up into working position.

2. Using the plastic needle pusher pictured, or your fingers if you don't have one, push half the needles back into non-working position.

3. With the correct yarn threaded and a suitable stitch size selected, take the carriage across the needles to lay in the yarn.

4. Now you want to add some weight to the yarn, so hang your cast-on comb onto the yarn that is laid into the needles and then hang weights onto it.

5. Check that the comb isn't caught on the needle bed anywhere. An easy way to do this is to push the comb and see if it swings freely.

6. When you're happy that the comb is hung correctly, move the carriage back across to knit stitches onto the needles in working position.

7. Now push the other half of the needles back into working position, making sure you have the right number of needles in total.

8. Move the carriage across the knitting area to lay yarn into the empty needles that have just been pushed up.

9. Take the carriage across again to form knitted stitches on all the needles. You're now ready to knit your swatch.

Quick Cast-on with Ravel Cord

This cast-on is perfect if you don't have a cast-on comb; in this case, you will usually have a ravel cord with the machine. It can also be useful if you are working with a tricky yarn – something that is prone to snapping or a fancy yarn. This method gives you an open cast-on with live stitches on the first knitted row that will unravel from the bottom if pulled.

1. To cast on with the ravel cord, start by selecting the knitting width on your machine, remembering to centre over the zero. Push all the needles you want to knit over up into working position.

2. With the yarn in the carriage and the tension set correctly for that yarn, take the carriage over the needles in working position.

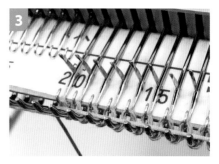

3. Take the ravel cord and lay it across the yarn loops, making sure it goes between the needle hooks and the gate pegs.

4. The ravel cord must pass round each gate peg at the edge of the knitting area to hold down all the stitches.

5. Now you need to put some take-down tension on the knitting by pulling down on the ravel cord before you knit across.

6. When you are happy that the cord is in the right place, you can take the carriage across to knit your first row.

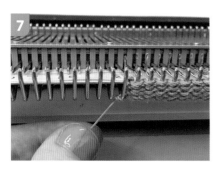

7. The cast-on is now complete, but you need to keep hold of the ravel cord and knit enough rows to allow you to add weights to the fabric.

8. Now you are ready to attach the weights to your knitting and carry on with the fabric. Pull the cord out from the knitting and attach weights.

E-Wrap Cast-on

This is the cast-on that I use the most, as it gives a neat, closed edge to the knitted fabric. It can be a bit fiddly when you are first learning but, like anything, it gets easier with practice. It is called an e-wrap because the yarn looks like a lower-case e when it's wrapped round the needles.

You will start with your carriage on the opposite side of the knitting to your yarn. If you are right-handed, you will usually wrap left to right, so start with the carriage on the right and yarn on the left. Left-handers will wrap from right to left so will start with the carriage on the left and yarn on the right.

1. E-wrap cast-on. Again, start by selecting the knitting width on your machine, remembering to centre over the zero. Push all the needles you want to use as far out as they will go and make sure the latches are open.

2. Now secure the yarn to the machine on the side from which you will be starting your cast-on. You can do this by tying the yarn to a clamp or the leg of the table your machine is on.

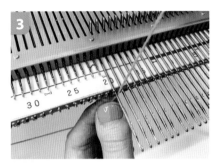

3. To start, wrap the yarn around the first needle at the opposite side of your selection to your carriage. Holding the yarn underneath the needle with one hand, bring it up between the first and second needles on the chosen side of your needle selection.

4. While keeping hold of the yarn under the needles with one hand, pass the yarn back over then under the stem of the first needle using your other hand. This motion will wrap the yarn around the first needle.

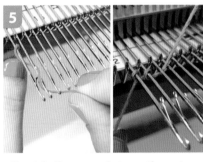

5. Now take the yarn up between the next two needles, then use the same motion to wrap the yarn round the second needle. It is important not to wrap too tightly around the stem of the needle, as it needs room to pass over the hook to form a stitch.

6. Repeat this e-wrapping process all the way to the end, wrapping the yarn around each needle in turn, holding onto the yarn under the needles with one hand and wrapping it around the needles with the other.

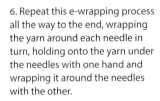

continued on the following page

7. Do this until you get to the last needle, then simply wrap this one in the same way as all the previous needles, bringing the yarn up at the edge of the knitting area.

8. Take the yarn and place it into the yarn-feeder slot on your carriage, make sure you close the feeder slot after inserting the yarn. At this point, also check that the stitch size is set correctly for this yarn.

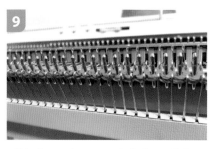

9. Take the carriage across to knit your first row. Now you could hang the comb and weights on to the fabric straight away. Make sure the teeth go into the fabric and don't get caught on the needle bed, then add weights.

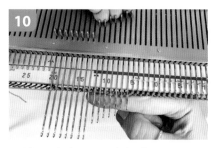

10. Alternatively, you can knit a few more rows before inserting the comb, making sure you push all the needles up into their top position before knitting across on these rows. When you have enough knitting, hang the comb into the fabric.

11. Whichever option you choose, it's important to insert the comb correctly, making sure it's through the fabric, and to hang the weights onto it before continuing to knit your sample.

Double E-Wrap Cast-on

This cast-on method uses what you have learnt in the e-wrap cast-on but adds another step to create a more solid cast-on, forming the first row of stitches as part of the cast-on. This method gives a stable, closed cast-on edge.

I have worked the right-handed way for the cast-on shown here. If you are left-handed, simply tie the yarn on the right-hand side of the knitting area and have the carriage on the left, as for the single e-wrap cast-on.

1. Double e-wrap cast-on. Again, select the knitting width on your machine, remembering to centre over the zero. Push all the needles you want to use as far out as they will go and make sure the latches are open.

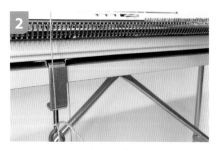

2. Now you've got the needles ready, secure the yarn at the side of the machine where you will be starting your cast-on. You can do this by tying the yarn to a clamp or the leg of the table your machine is on.

3. Start as you did for the e-wrap cast-on, wrapping the yarn around the first needle at the far left of your selection, then bringing the yarn up between the next two needles.

4. Now take the yarn over both the needle the yarn is next to and the needle that has yarn wrapped round it, making sure the yarn sits firmly in the top section above the latch on the wrapped needle so that a stitch can be formed.

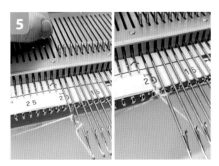

5. With the hand that isn't holding the yarn, pull the needle with the yarn laid into the hook away from you. When you do this, the yarn laid in will be caught and the loop on the needle will force the latch closed, forming a stitch.

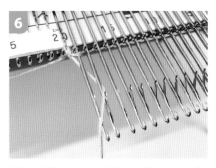

6. Repeat this process, bringing the yarn under the next two needles along and up, then lay it over two needles. Always make sure it sits in the upper part of the first of the two needles, above the latch.

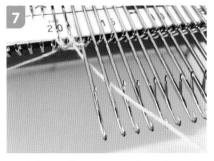

7. Pull the needle with yarn laid into the hook back to form the stitch. Take care to pull all the needles back to the same point; this action is forming your first row of stitches so you want it to be as even as possible.

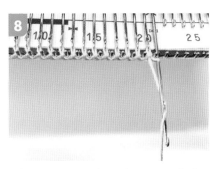

8. Repeat steps 6 and 7 until you get to the last needle. To make this stitch, simply lay the yarn into the top section of the needle, above the latch, and push the needle away from you to form the last stitch in your cast-on.

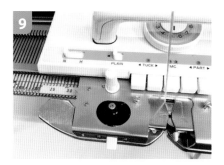

9. Take the yarn and place it into the yarn-feeder slot on your carriage, making sure you close the feeder after inserting the yarn. At this point, also check that the stitch size is set correctly for this yarn.

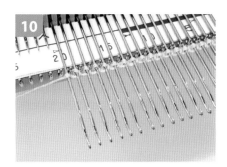

10. Before you knit across, push all the needles up into the position they started in, to allow the stitches that have been formed by hand to pass easily over the needles. Take the carriage across to knit your first row, then add your comb/weights.

11. As with the e-wrap cast-on, if you want to knit more rows before adding the comb and/or weights to the fabric, you can do – just remember to push the needles up into their topmost position before every knitted row.

Chain Stitch Cast-on

This is a cast-on that's perfect for the crocheters out there because you're forming chain stitches using the latch hook tool over the needles that you want to knit onto. If you want to get a closed edge but struggle with e-wrapping, this one is for you.

1. Chain stitch cast-on. As before, select the knitting width on your machine, remembering to centre over the zero. Push all the needles you want to use as far up as they will go and make sure the latches are open.

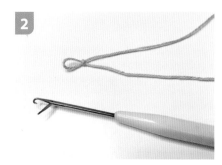

2. Make a slipknot in the end of the yarn you are using to cast on and have your latch tool ready. If you don't have one, you can use a latch needle.

3. Place the slipknot onto the latch tool and bring it up between the first and second needles at one edge of your needle selection. Ensure your carriage is at the other end.

4. Bring the yarn over the top of the first needle and place it in the hook of the latch tool, making sure it's caught.

5. Pull the latch tool down to form the first stitch around the first needle, take it under the next needle along and bring it up between the next two needles.

6. Repeat steps 4 and 5, bringing the yarn over the needle into the hook of the latch tool, pulling it down to form a stitch then moving the tool along.

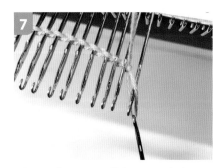

7. Repeat this process all the way to the last needle in your chosen knitting area. When you get to this needle, slip the loop from the tool onto the needle.

8. Now take the yarn over the last needle and thread it into the machine carriage's yarn feeder.

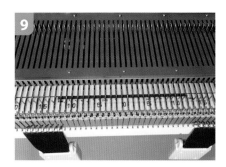

9. Knit across to complete your cast-on, add comb/weights as desired and continue to knit.

CHANGING COLOURS

Stripes are one of the staples of knit design: there is so much you can do with a handful of colours and a good stripe design. Before we get carried away designing the best stripe you've ever seen, let's look at how to stripe using two yarns.

Here you have two options for what to do when you swap your colours over: you can either cut the yarn, or just put it to rest while you use the other one. If you cut the yarn, you will have ends to work in, while if you put the yarn to rest, it will travel up the edge of the fabric.

In the picture you can see that where the stripes are narrow, the yarn travelling up the side is not very noticeable. Therefore, as a general rule, if I'm knitting narrow stripes I just put the yarn to rest, but if it's a big block of colour I cut it. You need to learn both ways because, once you start bringing in more colours, you will have to cut the yarns to replace them, as most knitting machines just have two feeders.

Here I have knitted the exact same stripe on both samples, but on the left one I have cut the yarns and on the other I have put them to rest.

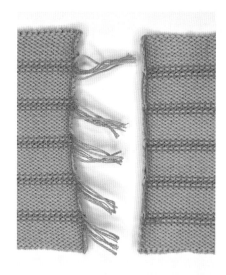

Resting the Yarn

To swap between colours using this method, simply put one yarn to rest while knitting the other. On my knitting machine, there is a small groove at the very end of the needle bed where I put my yarn when I'm not using it, but if you haven't got one of these, you can hook it under the corner of the machine.

1. After knitting the number of rows you want for your first stripe, take the yarn you are using out of the carriage and hook it into the groove on your machine on the same side on which it is threaded up.

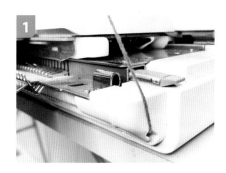

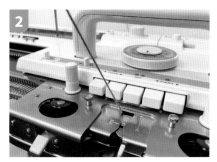

2. To start knitting with your second yarn, you first need to thread this yarn into the feeder on the machine and secure it in place.

3. Knit across with this yarn and work as many rows as you like, ending with the carriage at the side where the first yarn is resting.

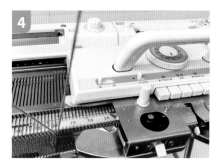

4. You are now ready to swap the yarns. Remove the second yarn from the feeder and the resting yarn from the groove.

continued on the following page

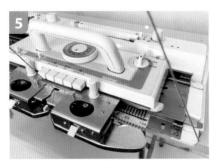

5. Swap the yarns' positions, making sure the twist in the yarn sits next to the fabric; put the second yarn to rest and the first yarn back in the feeder.

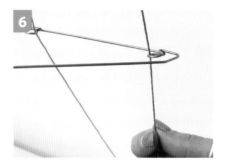

6. At this point, the yarn that has been resting may have some slack on it; to remove this, pull the yarn back towards the cone to tighten it up before knitting across.

7. Now knit the desired number of rows in this yarn, then repeat steps 4 to 6 to keep swapping yarns for the remainder of your knitted swatch.

Cutting the Yarn

To swap between colours using this method, cut the yarn you have just been using, place it in the clip on the tension mast and introduce the other colour. This leaves you with ends to work in, but is a useful technique if you are working with large stripes or more than two colours. The finishing section at the end of this chapter explains how to work these ends in while you are knitting; it's easy and a good habit to get into.

1. Take the yarn you have been using out of the carriage and cut it around 10cm (4in) from the edge needle. Remember to hold onto the yarn above where you are cutting.

2. When the yarn is cut, place the end back into the clip on the yarn mast (or equivalent on your machine).

3. Now take the new colour yarn and thread it into the yarn feeder. Once the yarn has been threaded, hold onto the end of it while knitting across rather than tying it, to reduce excess waste.

4. That's all there is to it: simply cut the yarn when you no longer want to use it, put that to rest in the clip, then thread the new yarn in when you want to knit with it.

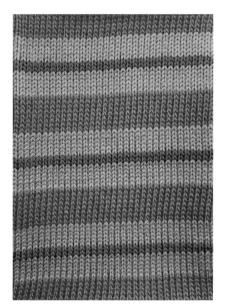

Swatch showing striping using three colours.

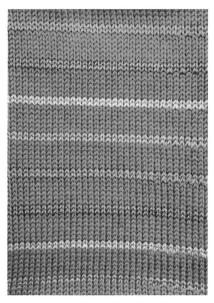

Here a multicolour stripe has been created by changing yarns more times throughout the knitting.

This sample shows how adding a textured yarn can change the look of a simple striped fabric.

You can add more colours to a piece of knitting by swapping any yarn out for a new one. A three-colour stripe where you keep one colour throughout and swap the other every time you change is an easy way to add interest to a stripe. To do this, just remove one yarn from the machine after cutting it and replace it with the new colour, repeating this whenever you want to swap colours. You will notice that this process can leave you with a lot of loose ends (see the Finishing section at the end of this chapter).

When working with stripes, you will want to keep count of the number of rows you are knitting in each colour, especially if you are working on a swatch for a new stripe design. It is surprising how much difference knitting two rows can make to the look of a stripe. Use your row counter (if you have one) to keep track, but you will also want to make a note of the number of rows of each colour to save having to count them if you want to use this stripe design again.

Once you have mastered changing yarns, you can have a go at bringing in more colours. It takes a little more time to create a multicolour stripe but it can be really effective. Have a go at designing your own stripe/colour sequence.

As well as using different colours, you can stripe using different qualities of yarn. A textured stripe is a quick and easy way to add interest to the surface of a knitted fabric. Remember, you can also mix yarns together to blend colours – you don't always have to work with solid colour.

THE TRANSFER TOOL

There is so much you can do with a transfer tool! I'm introducing it here so you can learn how to use it, experiment with it a bit, then use it to cast off. The tool we will be looking at here is the single-end transfer tool, but you will probably also have a double- and triple-end tool with your machine, and we will use these later on when we come to shaping.

A simple transfer tool with two prongs at one end and one at the other.

How to Use the Transfer Tool

The main job of this tool is to move stitches in a few simple steps.

1. Place the eye of the transfer tool over the hook of your chosen latch needle.

2. Pull the needle towards you with the transfer tool until the stitch passes the latch.

3. Push the needle away from you; the stitch will travel back up the needle and close the latch.

4. Keep pushing the needle until the stitch moves from the needle onto the transfer tool.

5. Raise the transfer tool from the needle and the stitch is moved away. You can now move the transfer tool over to the adjacent needle, placing the eye of the tool on the hook of this needle.

6. Tip the tool up and away from you towards the machine to transfer the stitch from the tool onto the needle.

7. Your stitch has now been moved to the next needle and the transfer is complete.

Transferring to Create Holes and Ladders

When you have moved the stitch, you can create either a hole or a ladder in the fabric depending on the position of the needle. These methods can be used to create a huge range of decorative effects in fabrics. If this is a technique you enjoy, you can have a lot of fun designing your own lace transfer patterns, but for now we're just going to look at the basics and practise using the tool.

Making Holes

To make a hole in the fabric, simply transfer a stitch using the process above, and place the empty needle in working position.

When you then knit across, this needle will catch the yarn and start to knit again. On the first row, the yarn will just lay into the needle hook as it does on the first cast-on row. Knit another row and you will see a stitch form on this needle; the empty needle is now knitting and a small hole will have formed in the fabric.

That's all there is to it. You can practise this by having a go at making a simple pattern using holes. If you have a certain shape in mind, make sure you're thinking about which direction you are transferring the stitches in, as it will be visible on the surface of the fabric.

Making Ladders

To make a ladder, follow the same steps for transferring a stitch as before, but put the empty needle into non-working position.

Now when you knit across, the yarn won't catch on the needle, which means an intentional ladder will form in the fabric.

You can knit as many rows as you like with a needle out of action to create a long ladder; whenever you want the ladder to stop, simply bring the empty needle back into working position.

You will notice, if you continue to knit a few rows, that the end of the ladder looks like a lace hole. If you don't mind this effect, you can just end the ladder in this way, but if you would rather the top of the ladder look more like the bottom, simply lift the bump of the previous stitch on one side of the ladder onto the empty needle before knitting across to finish the ladder. Putting this stitch on the needle closes the ladder manually before you take the carriage across, which means you won't have the hole at the top of the ladder.

As with holes, you can also create decorative patterns using ladders. Wider ladders and moving ladders can both be created by transferring more stitches or different stitches, and taking those needles out of working position. Have a play around and see what you can create.

The stitch has been transferred to the next needle and the empty needle placed in working position.

The empty needle has picked up the yarn on this row.

The previously empty needle now has a knitted stitch on it.

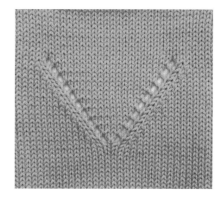

Here the stitches have been moved in different directions to create a V shape; a double-pronged tool has been used to move two stitches by one position leaving one empty needle, and you can see the direction the stitches have been moved.

Making Ladders

The stitch has been transferred to the next needle and the empty needle pushed down out of working position.

The yarn is floating over this area because the needle is not in working position.

The yarn is knitting back onto the needle, ending the ladder.

The ladder has a visible hole at the top of it.

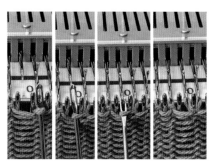

Use your transfer tool to lift the bump of the previous stitch from the adjacent needle onto the empty needle before knitting across.

The hole has been closed by placing a stitch here.

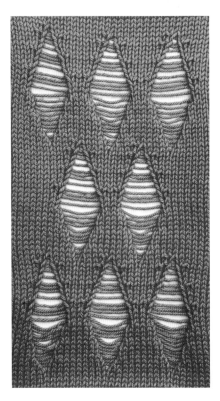

Shaped ladders created by transferring stitches and taking more needles out of working position, then bringing them back in to knit.

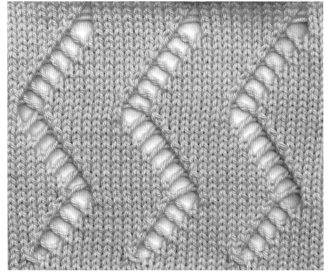

Moving ladders created by transferring the stitch next to the empty needle by one position when bringing the empty needle back into working position.

CASTING OFF

There are quite a number of different ways that are used to cast off (sometimes referred to as 'binding off') on a knitting machine. Below are the methods I find work best; two of these involve making a closed edge and the third gives you live stitches, but all are useful to know. As with the cast-on, it's a good idea to have a go at all three and keep a swatch of each for reference.

Transfer Tool Cast-off

This method uses the transfer tool, which is why we have already practised using it because this process can be a bit fiddly. With this method, we are taking the stitches behind the gate pegs on the machine; if your machine doesn't have these, don't worry, as you can replace some cast-off edge stitches back onto the needles to help keep the tension even. The photographs here show the kind of finish you can expect using this method.

Closed edge created using the transfer tool cast-off method.

1. The first thing you need to do is remove your yarn from the carriage. Then pull the yarn through so you have a slack length of yarn to work with.

2. Using your transfer tool, take the first stitch at the same side as your yarn and transfer it onto the next needle, taking it behind the gate peg.

3. You now have two stitches on the second needle and the first needle is empty. To move on with this cast-off you need to make a new stitch.

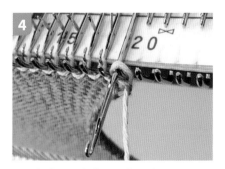

4. To do this, push the needle with two stitches on towards you. The stitches will push the latch open; both stitches then need to travel past the open latch onto the stem of the needle.

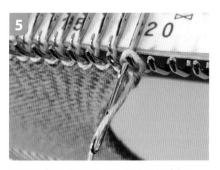

5. Now place the yarn into the hook of this needle, making sure it is lying at the top of the needle in front of the latch.

6. With the yarn in one hand, use your other hand to push the needle away from you. Keep pushing the needle away from you to pull the yarn through the stitches on the needle and form a new stitch.

continued on the following page

7. Now you have formed a new stitch on this needle, you are ready to transfer it to the next needle, remembering to pass it behind the gate peg.

8. Continue this pattern of making a new stitch then transferring it until you reach the last needle on your knitting area.

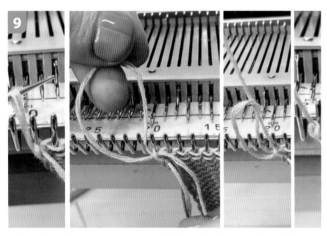

9. Simply cut the yarn around 10cm (4in) from the last needle, pull the loop off the needle and thread the yarn end through it to make a knot.

10. Your cast-off is now complete, so you can remove the weights from the fabric and lift if off the gate pegs.

Latch Tool Cast-off

This method gives a similar finish to the transfer tool cast-off but is done using the latch tool instead. It can be easier to make a slightly looser cast-off using this method. It is important to try this technique because this is the cast-off method that is used when you come to joining pieces (linking) on your knitting machine.

Closed edge created using the latch tool cast-off method.

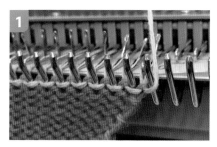

1. Remove the yarn from the feeder in the carriage and place it on the outside of the gate peg at the edge of your knitting area.

2. Now push all the working needles all the way up into holding position – this will open all the latches, making the process easier.

3. Take hold of the yarn with one hand and the latch tool with the other; hold the yarn back behind the gate pegs, keeping your thumb free.

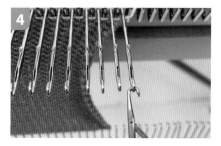

4. Place the hook of the tool into the hook of the first needle. Make sure it's in securely, as the stitch will pass from the needle onto the tool.

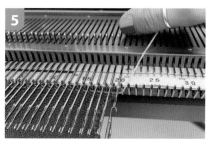

5. Using the thumb of the hand that is holding the yarn, pull the needle with the tool hooked onto it back down the machine away from you.

6. Keep pulling the needle until the stitch has opened the latch on the tool and moved from the needle up the stem of the latch tool.

7. Making sure the yarn is behind the gate peg, place it into the latch tool then pull the tool towards you to make a stitch.

8. Now you have a stitch on the latch tool, you will push the next needle back to upper working position before hooking the latch tool onto it so the stitch doesn't get stretched.

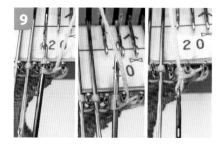

9. Keep following the same steps, pulling the needle back to transfer the stitch from the needle onto the tool, then making a new stitch.

10. Remember, the stitch is passing in front of the gate pegs and the yarn behind, helping to create an even bind-off edge to the knitting.

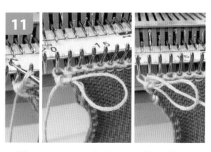

11. When you get to the last needle, make a new stitch, then simply cut the yarn and take it through the loop as you did for the latch tool cast-off.

12. Your cast-off is now complete; just remove the weights from the fabric and lift if off the gate pegs.

Removing Knitting using Waste Yarn

This method is different, and much quicker! You would only use this if you want to keep live stitches at the end of your knitted piece, so is often used for garments where you have stitches to hook back onto the machine for attaching a trim, joining panels together and so on.

Knitted sample with waste yarn at top.

1. To set up for cast-off with waste yarn, knit the last row of your knitted fabric at a slightly looser tension to the rest of it; this will make the stitches easier to work with when you are hooking them back on or linking them.

2. Now you need to swap to your waste yarn; always use a smooth yarn that is easy to unravel. It's a good idea to keep a cone of waste yarn that you can unravel the waste back onto and reuse.

3. Knit between ten and twenty rows with the waste yarn. You might knit more or less, but as a general rule you want just enough fabric to hold onto/handle.

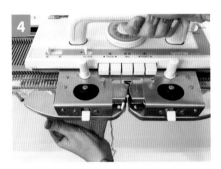

4. When you have knitted the desired number of rows, remove the waste yarn from the feeder and knit across without any yarn to remove the fabric from the machine.

5. When the fabric comes off the machine, take care to cut the waste yarn close to the top of the fabric so that it doesn't unravel.

FINISHING

So, you have made a knitted swatch with a beautiful cast-off edge, but the fabric is curling up and you've got some loose ends hanging off it. Don't worry, we are now going to go through how to work the ends of yarn in and some finishing methods to flatten out that fabric and get the fibres to relax.

Working in Ends

We will start with working in loose ends on the knitting machine. When you have cut the yarn to swap it for a new one, simply push a number of needles at the edge of your knitting up into hold position and weave the yarn under and over these needles to secure it before knitting with the new colour. Then on the next row, do the same thing with the new colour to secure this in the knitting too.

This weaving technique works well when knitting simple stripes, for example, but sometimes it won't be suitable and you will be left with ends to sew in, so it's important to know how to do that too.

There are two main ways to work ends into the fabric when the fabric is off the machine: either with a sewing needle or a latch tool. I usually use the latch tool, but sometimes the yarn is a bit too thin or the stitches too tight for this, so it's good to know both methods.

Sewing in Ends
For this you will need a sewing needle that is big enough to thread the yarn into and some small, sharp scissors.

End of yarn woven through at the edge of the knitting after the last row has been knitted in this colour.

The end woven through after the first course of this second colour has been knitted.

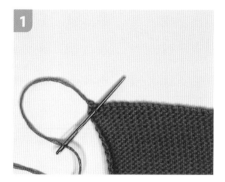

1. Find the end that you want to work into the fabric and thread it into the needle.

2. Now take the needle through the back of the knitted loops by passing it under each stitch one at a time.

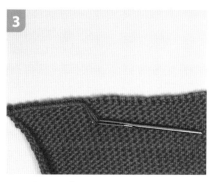

3. Do this over five–ten stitches to make sure the yarn is secured into the back of the fabric.

4. When you're happy with the finish, unthread the needle and trim any excess yarn.

Using a Latch Tool to Secure Ends

For this you will need a latch tool, or a spare knitting machine needle if you don't have a tool, and some small, sharp scissors.

Find the end that you want to work into the fabric, and on the row that the yarn is coming from, insert your latch tool under a number of bottom stitch loops on the back of the fabric; between five and ten is usually enough.

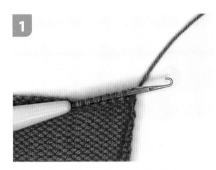

1. Insert the latch tool through the bottom stitch loops on the back of the fabric.

2. Now pick the yarn up in the hook of the latch tool.

3. Pull the latch needle back through the loops, bringing your yarn end through with it.

4. When the yarn is secure, trim the end of it to neaten the back of the fabric.

Fabric Finishing

You have completed the knitting when you take the fabric off the machine, but the fabric still needs to be 'finished'. This is the term used for the various processes that take your fabric from being fresh off the machine to being ready to wear or use in the garment/product you are creating; it relaxes the fibres and stitches and allows the fabric to be set to its desired size/shape.

Washing

Washing of fabrics is essential if you are planning on washing the finished piece because all fibres will react to being washed and many experience some shrinkage. Some yarns, such as lambswool, should be washed for initial shrinkage to take place and for the fibres to 'full', giving the fabric a softer feel, whereas other wool or wool blend yarns may have been developed so they won't shrink; I would recommend washing them anyway.

When washing a fabric swatch or a finished garment, consistency is key. If you hand-wash your swatch, then hand-wash the finished garment in water that is the same temperature with exactly the same soap or detergent. If you use a cold machine wash on the sample, do the same for a finished garment.

If you are working with a felting wool, unless you want the fabric to felt, use a very low temperature to wash it and a small amount of wool detergent. If machine washing, use a low spin so the fabric is not agitated too much; if washing by hand, gently squeeze out the excess water, taking care not to pull the fabric out of shape, before blocking it into shape.

Blocking

This essential part of the finishing process helps to set your fabric to the required size. To do this successfully you will need some blocking mats and pins.

When blocking knitting, you are simply pinning the fabric to the desired size, wetting it to help the fibres move into the desired position, and letting it dry in the new position. The most important things are that you pin it to the right size, and that you don't stretch it out of shape while it is wet.

If you have washed your fabric, you can then block it while it's wet. If you aren't washing it, you can wet the fabric with a spray bottle or a steam iron. The first step is always to pin your knitted piece out to the desired size on your blocking mat/s, making sure you use enough pins to give the fabric a nice even edge; if you just use a few pins down one edge you will end up with an uneven wavy edge to the fabric.

Blocking mat with blocking pins.

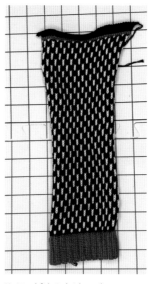
Knitted fabric laid on the mat before blocking.

Misting

Using a spray bottle, simply spray the fabric until it is damp through. The wetter the fabric, the more likely it is to retain the shape when you remove the pins. Leave the fabric to dry completely before doing so.

Steaming

With the fabric pinned in place on a blocking mat, hold the steam iron just above it and allow the steam to pass through the fabric. Apply as much steam as you like, but always keep the iron **off** the fabric surface. I find this method a bit more effective than misting as it is applying heat as well as water, but with that in mind, be careful when steaming fibres that could shrink. Leave the fabric to dry completely before removing the pins.

You can see from the images here how much difference blocking can make to the resulting fabric.

TENSION SWATCH

We have been through lots of processes, from casting on to finishing fabrics, but before you can jump into your first project, we need to think about tension swatches.

The purpose of this book is not just to give you patterns and projects to follow, but to teach you the things you need to know to be able to design your own knits, and tension swatches are an essential part of that. The tension swatch will always be knitted in the same yarn and stitch that your finished piece will be knitted in. When you move onto projects with more than one kind of stitch, for example a jumper with a rib trim or contrasting sleeves, you will need to do a tension swatch for each different fabric.

The tension swatch needs to be big enough to measure from, so around 15cm (6in) wide. I usually use fifty needles on my machine, but this will vary depending on the thickness of yarn and the kind

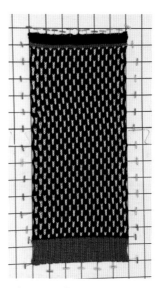
Fabric pinned to size using blocking pins.

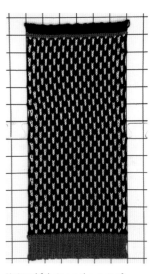
Knitted fabric on the mat after blocking.

of machine you are using. Before making the tension swatch you will use for calculations, you will usually want to try the yarn and stitch you are using at a few different stitch sizes to get the desired feel of the fabric. To do this, thread up the yarn that you will be using for the project – we will call this the main yarn – as well as a contrasting colour, then follow these steps:

1. Cast on and knit around ten rows in the main yarn.
2. Change to the contrast yarn and knit two rows to give a contrast stripe.
3. Return to the main yarn and knit as many rows as you want in your first stitch size to give you the feel of the fabric. When you have knitted nearly enough in that yarn, record the stitch size used. You can do this on the fabric by making a number of transfer holes in the knitting that matches the number of the stitch size you have been using, or simply make a note of the size. If doing the latter, it can be helpful to pin the note/s to the finished swatch.
4. Swap to the contrast yarn and knit two rows to make a clear division between the areas with different stitch sizes.
5. Knit a number of rows in your main yarn using a different stitch size. Repeat steps 3 and 4 for as many stitch sizes as you want to test in that yarn. Remember to finish the fabric, by washing or steaming it, before deciding which stitch size to go with.

When you have decided which stitch size gives you the best quality of fabric, you are ready to knit a separate tension swatch. Use the same process, but this time only using the chosen stitch size, putting in a contrast stripe around an inch from the beginning and end of the fabric, and remember to record the stitch size using your chosen method.

I usually knit between fifty and a hundred rows for my tension swatch. The number of rows you knit will depend on the yarn and machine you are using; knitting in a fine yarn on a standard-gauge machine will make a much smaller swatch than a thick yarn on a chunky machine. Don't forget to finish the swatch using the appropriate method for the yarn before taking these measurements.

Now you have the tension swatch using your chosen yarn and knit technique/s at your chosen stitch size, you will use it as the basis for all your calculations for your project. Before you can do this, you need to work out how many stitches and rows there are in this fabric per centimetre/inch.

Swatch trying out different tensions before making the final tension swatch for this project.

Tension swatch knitted over fifty needles with a hundred rows knitted at stitch size 4.

Tension Swatch Calculations

Let's start with the number of rows. Depending on whether you are working in centimetres or inches, take your swatch and use two pins to mark an area of 10cm or 4in vertically on the fabric; you will be counting the rows in this area.

Using the head of a pin to help you keep track of where you are, count the number of rows between the two pins to get the number of rows over the 10cm (4in). In the example here, I counted forty-two rows between these pins. To get the number of rows per cm/inch, simply divide this number by 10 or 4:

- 42 rows by 10 = 4.2 rows per cm
- 42 rows divided by 4 = 10.5 rows per inch

Keep these numbers to two decimal places because you will have to multiply them back up later to calculate how many rows you need to knit, and if you round them up or down you lose some of the accuracy. You can't knit a fraction of a stitch, so the number will get rounded to the nearest whole number later in the process.

Measuring the stitches is a little different. Due to the edge of the knitting rolling and the quality of the stitches at the edges being different to those in the centre, you don't measure the whole piece. Select an area in the middle of the knitted piece to count the stitches in. I use a ruler or tape measure to find the area that I want to use, then place a pin at either end of it. I usually work over 10cm (4in), so:

- 34 stitches divided by 10 = 3.4 stitches per cm
- 34 stitches divided by 4 = 8.5 stitches per inch

We now have the values for this knitted fabric, which are:
- 8.5 stitches and 10.5 rows per inch
- 3.4 stitches and 4.2 rows per cm

When you have been through this process with your tension swatch, you can then apply these values to any calculations for any project you carry out using this yarn at this specific tension. Remember to make sure the fabric is also finished in the same way as the tension swatch.

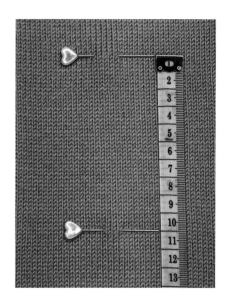

Pins used to mark 10cm (4in) of knitted rows.

Marking a 10cm-wide (4in) area using pins to measure the number of stitches.

Jonathan 'Jonny' Le – Jonnyknits

Jonny in the studio.

Knitting the fabric for a knitted sculpture.

I'm Jonathan Le and I run Jonnyknits, a brand of soft knitted friends I knit from home, just outside Los Angeles, California.

What brought you to machine knitting and where did you learn?

I studied illustration at RISD (The Rhode Island School of Design) but was constantly working in different physical media because I hated working digitally and my laptop was fried at the time. I tried out stop-motion animation, painting, ceramics and woodworking before I finally arrived at textiles. During my junior year, I took an Intro to Machine Knitting class because I was living with a lot of textile students at the time and I thought, why not? Definitely did not do my research, because I confused weaving with knitting and assumed we would be working on looms. I had no idea what machine knitting was and had never hand knitted prior, so I really struggled those first two weeks! But that wonderful class opened my eyes to this amazing machine and I have been knitting since, learning more advanced techniques via very enthusiastic Facebook groups and grainy but insightful YouTube videos.

Can you tell us about the knitting machines you use now and why they are the right machines for your practice?

My main machine is a Brother KH864, an old standard-gauge domestic punch-card knitting machine. Their name is Julie and they have served me very well over the past few years. I find the

punch-card machines to be very reliable and I love the simplicity of the mechanical punch-card mechanism. I also have a Brother KH930 electronic machine, but I don't currently utilise any of the electronic elements in making my work. Finally, I have a Brother KE100 motor drive, which pushes the knitting carriage back and forth and saves me a great deal of elbow grease and time.

How about your design process – what inspires you?

I draw daily in my diary and flesh out my characters in my sketchbook. I do some simple colouring to figure out the shape and ideas, and then I put it on Photoshop for some more flexibility. I love, *love* old school commercial illustrators like Mary Blair and Alexander Girard, funky and unusual colours and things that make me laugh.

When you've got your inspiration, how do you take it from idea to the finished product?

After I'm happy with my design, I figure out the maths and pattern in my sketchbook and draw accordingly. I am wrong 75 per cent of the time so I'm constantly adjusting. Doing tension swatches prior to knitting helps a ton to measure and visualise the final product. After the knitting, I wash, stuff and sew the sculptures closed. The last stage is felting and embroidery, along with coming up with an appropriate name for my new soft little friend.

Do you have any favourite yarns that you like to work with?
I love using lambswool and merino yarns because they are buttery to work with on the machine and their behaviour is very predictable. I love using bright and bold colours!

This chapter has been all about getting started with the machine. Do you have any preferred cast-on/cast-off methods or any advice on the first steps of using a knitting machine?
The e-wrap cast on was the simplest cast-on to understand when I first started, and the latch tool cast-off was the easiest method to cast off. Nowadays, there are many videos on YouTube fully explaining these processes, so I would recommend following them very slowly. Make sure the yarn tension on the yarn mast and knitting carriage is correct. It will take some experience to determine what feels appropriate, but it should feel smooth. One mistake I made all the time when starting out was forgetting to close the gate on the carriage. It is devastating when the piece you've been working on for hours drops to the ground because the yarn escaped your carriage, so make sure it's closed! Also, the machine prefers coned yarn, so if your yarn is on a hank or a ball, make sure to wind it onto something before feeding it into the machine.

What about projects for beginners? What kinds of things did you make when you first started out?
In class, I made small swatches for weeks before starting a real project. They were very simple, just testing out all the different possible techniques, textures and yarns. A good first 'real' project would be a scarf or, if you are feeling extra adventurous, a blanket. You can mix and match all the different ideas you formed in your beginning swatches to make something really unique. Once you understand the basic mechanics of the machine, you can move to more complex projects that require shaping and finishing.

Do you have any advice for people who are learning to use a knitting machine? Is there anything you wish you had known when you were starting out?
There are many resources and communities online. I found a great Facebook group run by very friendly people from around the world who are very excited to share the ideas and experience they have hoarded over the years. This hobby is definitely niche and difficult to learn, so it is great to connect with people who have truly seen it all. Machine knitting can be very frustrating, but when you persevere and figure it out, it is extremely rewarding.

Characters in progress.

Jonny's finished creations.

Where can people find your work?
- @jonnyknits
- @jonnyknits
- www.jonnyknits.com

Bubble Yum Colour-Block Scarf

Finished striped scarf with pompoms.

Tension swatch that also tests yarn colours and proportions.

Now you have learned the basics, it is time for your first project. This colour-block design can be made in any yarns you like, it's a super-easy project and at the end of it you will have made something that you can wear. I used a four-ply merino wool from Yeoman Yarns in pink, red and turquoise to knit this project.

You will need:

- Yarns to knit your scarf
- Tape measure
- Pins
- Calculator
- Blocking mat/s and pins
- Sewing needle
- Cardboard or pom-pom maker
- Sharp scissors

TENSION SWATCH

When you have chosen the yarns that you would like to use, the first thing you need to do is make a tension swatch. I used the tension swatch not only to get my tension values, but also to see how the colours worked with each other and test out some different proportions.

If the yarns you're using are slightly different qualities, knit them all into the tension swatch in the same proportions you are planning on using them in the scarf. This project is a great way to put into practice the tension swatch knitting and calculating covered in this chapter.

Before you can knit the scarf, you need to work out how many needles you will be knitting over, and how many rows to knit. Following the steps outlined in the Tension Swatch section, calculate the stitches and rows per centimetre or inch in your tension swatch. Then simply work through the following steps to find out how many needles you need to cast on and how many rows you will knit. I like to use a notepad or Post-it notes to write these down on as I work them out, as I can easily take these notes to my machine to follow as I knit.

Width of Scarf

When calculating the width of any piece of knitting, you are working out the number of needles you will be knitting on. You can change the width if you want the scarf to be wider or narrower. I made mine 25cm (10in) wide.

Now, to get the number of needles you will need to cast on, multiply your stitches per cm/inch by the width of your scarf. Below are all my calculations in centimetres:

- Stitches per cm/inch × width of scarf in cm/inches = number of needles
- My calculation: 3.2 sts per cm × 25cm = 80 needles
- My tension was 3.2 stitches per cm and the scarf was 25cm wide, so I knitted it over eighty needles.

Length of Scarf

Now for the length of the scarf. My total length was 150cm. We need to break this down into blocks for the design. There were three block sizes used – small, medium and large – sized as follows:

- Small block = 5cm (2in)
- Medium block = 15cm (6in)
- Large block = 25cm (10in)

For each block, use your tension swatch values to work out how many rows you need to knit. Simply multiply your rows per cm/inch by the length of the block to get the number of rows you need to knit for that block:

- Rows per cm/inch × length of block in cm/inches = number of rows to knit for that block
- Calculation for medium block: 4.6 rows/cm × 15cm = 69 rows (rounded up to 70)
- Use this process for each colour block and note them down as 'small block = X rows' and so on, so you have this information to hand as you knit the scarf.

BLOCK COLOURS

The scarf design is made up of three different sizes of block as detailed above. These blocks are knitted in three different colours. In my design, pink is colour 1, red colour 2 and blue colour 3. The design is made up of nine blocks, and the block/colour patterning is as follows:

Block 1: Large, col 1
Block 2: Small, col 2
Block 3: Large, col 1
Block 4: Large, col 3
Block 5: Medium, col 1
Block 6: Small, col 3
Block 7: Large, col 2
Block 8: Medium, col 1
Block 9: Medium, col 3

Before you move to the machine, make a note of the rows and colours for each block so that you can follow it as you knit; this will be your knitting list.

Now you have worked out everything you need to knit the scarf and are ready to begin!

KNITTING THE SCARF

To knit the scarf, cast on your required number of needles using colour 1 and a closed cast-on method of your choice (I used the e-wrap cast-on). Then simply follow the block pattern using your own knitted row calculations from the above pattern. My knitting list was as follows:

Block 1: 116 rows, pink
Block 2: 24 rows, red
Block 3: 116 rows, pink
Block 4: 116 rows, blue
Block 5: 70 rows, pink
Block 6: 24 rows, blue
Block 7: 116 rows, red
Block 8: 70 rows, pink
Block 9: 70 rows, blue

To make it easier to keep track of the rows, I would recommend zeroing the row counter at each colour change. Due to the size of the knitted blocks, I cut the yarn when changing colours and wove the ends in as I knitted rather than having to work them in (*see* Finishing, right)

When you have knitted all nine colour blocks, you can cast off using your favourite closed cast-off method.

FINISHING

When the scarf is off the machine, wash and/or block it to finish the knitted fabric before adding the pom-poms. To make the pom-poms, use either colour 2 from your sequence to get a contrasting effect or mix all three colours together.

You can either use a pom-pom maker, or two ring-doughnut-shaped pieces of card a couple of centimetres bigger than you want the pom-poms to be. Holding the two pieces of card together, wrap yarn through the centre hole around the rims of both pieces, effectively tying them together. Keep going until you can fit no more yarn through the centre hole, then cut between the two donuts with your scissors. Pass a length of yarn between the two donuts around the bundle of fibres and tie it tightly. Fluff the cut ends into your pom-pom shape and (if necessary) trim to even out the surface, leaving the length of yarn you tied it with.

To attach the pom-poms, first gather the end of the scarf together using a large sewing needle and the same yarn you knitted that section with and secure the gather. Do this at both ends before adding a pom-pom to each end to complete the scarf. Use the long end you left when you tied the pom-pom to sew it onto the end of the scarf.

Gathering the end of the scarf.

Adding the pom-pom to the end of the scarf.

CHAPTER 3

PATTERN AND GARMENT CONSTRUCTION

In this chapter we are looking at adding pattern to your knitted fabrics. Punch cards are such a great tool, whether you use the cards that come with your machine or design your own, opening up a whole world of opportunity for knitted fabric design.

You can't work with pattern punch cards without considering colour, so we are also going to look at using colour in machine knitting. Towards the end of the chapter, we will also be looking at some hem and garment construction techniques that you will need to complete this chapter's project.

PUNCH CARDS

Most knitting machines come with a selection of punch cards; these can vary from simple patterns to pictorial images, and you can do so much with them. One punch-card design can provide you with many different fabrics by simply using different yarns with it.

You can also get punch cards for other fabric effects, such as lace and tuck stitches, but the ones we are looking at are pattern punch cards that allow you to knit patterns using two colours at a time, often referred to as Fair Isle pattern cards. These cards have solid areas and areas where holes have been punched out; when these are fed into the machine and knitted, one yarn will knit where holes are punched out and the other colour where there is solid card.

Pattern punch cards provided with a Brother knitting machine.

These swatches show how different fabrics can be created using the same punch card.

Pictorial punch cards are often designed to involve a colour change within the knitting of the card. This is a great way to get more colours involved in a design while only ever knitting with two colours in the machine at the same time.

Pictorial punch card using colour changes to create effects.

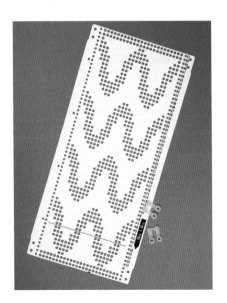

Punch card with clips.

Using Punch Cards

Most punch cards are the same width and you can use them in a range of domestic machines, but how you set up your machine to knit the punch card varies by machine manufacturer, so you will need to find the relevant instructions for your machine. One of the great things about pattern punch cards is that they repeat across your knitting area, and there is no limit to how many rows you can knit them for. You can also turn the punch card around to flip the design horizontally, vertically or both.

As well as the card, you will need clips to join the punch card to itself so that it can pass through the card reader continually. When you have these and you have chosen the two yarns you would like to knit with, you are ready to have a go at punch-card knitting.

Knitting with a Punch Card

1. Find the slot in the knitting machine in which to insert the punch card; make sure the card is straight when you insert it. You will feel the teeth inside the punch-card reader catch onto the holes in the edge of the card.
2. When you're happy that it's straight, roll the card through the reader using the knob or wheel (depending on the machine) until the same amount of punch card is showing at each side.
3. Making sure that you place the top of the card over the bottom, secure the card using the clips provided, then roll it through to the start line on the card. The start line is usually six rows into the pattern; the row that is knitting is not visible to you because it is inside the reader.
4. Now follow the instructions for your machine on how to knit using the punch card. This will usually involve a set-up row where you knit with just one of the two colours. This may seem strange, but it is correct – it is positioning the patterning devices in the carriage ready to knit the second colour on the next row. Remember to take your punch card off pause setting at the correct point for your knitting machine.
5. Once you have set up the punch card with the correct carriage settings and the second yarn colour in through the yarn feeder, simply keep knitting: the card will roll round and the pattern will knit.

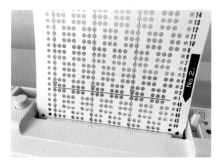

Punch card inserted straight and ready to feed through the punch-card reader.

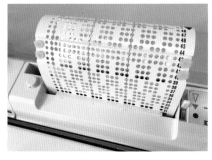

Punch card rolled through the reader and clipped together.

Set-up row of knitting with punch card.

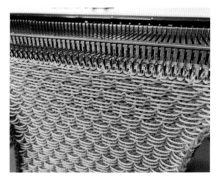

Fair Isle fabric knitting on the machine.

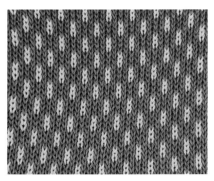

The front of the same fabric showing the pattern that has been knitted.

TOP TIP

When you are knitting a punch card, the yarns will often need a slightly different tension/stitch size setting to when they are knitted on their own – usually a few clicks higher on the stitch size dial, but this varies between yarns.

When knitting the fabric, you are looking at the back of the knitted fabric – the side where the yarns float over the fabric between the needles they are knitting on; the other side will show your pattern clearly.

When knitting with a punch card, you can stop the pattern and go back to knitting with one colour at any point. You will want to do this at the end of the fabric before you cast off, but you can also do it to create single colour stripes or blocks of colour within your design. To do this, disengage the punch-card function, take your second colour out of the carriage and knit with one colour. You could even introduce a third, contrasting colour here instead if you like.

Fair Isle knitted fabric with block-colour areas.

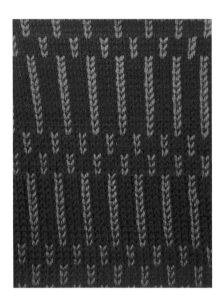

Fair Isle knitted fabric with elongated pattern sections.

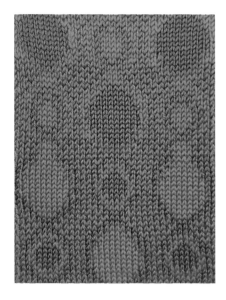

One pattern punch card has been used, with the main and contrast colours swapped over halfway through the swatch.

Another simple thing you can do to alter the pattern is to pause the punch card; this stops the card from rolling through until you change the setting again, making an elongated version of one row of the pattern. This can be a fun way to abstract the pattern in places. Some knitting machines also have the option to lengthen the whole punch card pattern by setting the machine so that the card turns every two knitted rows instead of every row. Have a play around and see how many different versions of the same pattern you can create.

Colour Combinations

We have looked at how to use the punch card, and a few things you can do to alter the pattern and overall effect. Another factor that can hugely change the visual effect of a pattern punch card is the colour choice.

Firstly, you can get different results by changing which yarn is the main and which is the contrast colour. I do this with any punch card I am using because until you try it out it is hard to visualise which will work best as the dominant colour. I like to knit a swatch and swap the colours over halfway through it; to do this, simply take both yarns out of the carriage then put them back in the opposite slots. Whichever yarn was in the feeder slot furthest from you will now be in the closer slot and vice versa.

As well as swapping yarns over, just using different colours with different levels of contrast can give varied effects. For example, a punch card knitted using black and white will have a very different aesthetic to the same one knitted using tonal shades of the same colour.

The same pattern punch card knitted using black and white, and tonal pinks.

Yarn Combinations

So far, all the examples of pattern punch cards have been knitted using single yarns, and they have mostly been smooth yarns. Another very easy way to create varied effects using pattern punch cards is to work with different yarn qualities. A patterned knitted fabric using two standard acrylic yarns will look very different to the same pattern knitted using a boucle yarn and a wool yarn.

As well as using fancy yarns, remember that you can combine different yarns to create a blended colour, as long as the thickness of the combined yarns isn't too much for your knitting machine.

Different looks created using textured yarn and standard yarn.

Blended colours created by combining yarns.

Elastic and mercerised cotton yarn knitted in the same sample creates a textured surface as well as providing stretch to the fabric. The right-hand image shows the fabric stretched out to show the pattern that has been knitted.

Felting wool and cotton yarn knitted in the same sample and felted gives an interesting surface.

Interesting effects can also be created by using finer yarns. If you use very fine yarn, you will see some of the floats (pieces of yarn on the reverse side of your knitting) through the fabric, which adds even more interest. As well as using different weights, colours and combinations of yarns, using different fibre types can also create interest. If you want to create surface interest, try a felting wool with a non-felting yarn and hot wash it to felt the wool. When you have acquired more experience, you might even want to try an elastic yarn to get an interesting surface texture and a more flexible fabric.

Designing Your Own

When you have gone through all the patterns that come with your knitting machine, you will probably be itching to design your own punch cards, and you can. All you need are some blank cards and a card punch. If you have a second-hand machine, the chances are there was a card punch with it, but if not, you can easily pick one up online.

Blank card and card punch.

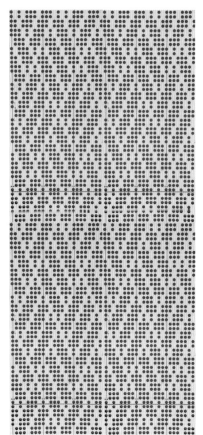

Existing pattern punch card showing how the edges of the design meet up.

At this point, you will have knitted a number of existing punch cards and understand the relationship between the pattern on the card and how it comes out when knitted. This is important because you need an idea of the scale of the pattern you want to create. Ideally, you will also have an idea of the yarns you will be using – as we now know, pattern scale and shape can be hugely affected by the yarn it is knitted with.

A tension swatch using the yarns you want to incorporate in your design and a punch card with a similar design density can be really helpful in working out your design. I always start with the tension swatch, using this to work out roughly how many stitches and rows I want the main motifs in the design to be.

You will also understand from using punch cards that where holes are punched out is where the secondary yarn will knit, and where there is solid punch card is where the main yarn will knit. Take this into consideration when planning the design, as the punched-out area is usually the design.

Now for the design. The punch card is twenty-four stitches wide and sixty rows long, so this is the area you will be designing in. If your repeat doesn't fit into the sixty rows, you can make it shorter, punch all the holes in the remaining rows out and clip the card together in a slightly different position, but if you can, it is simpler to make the pattern repeat within the sixty rows.

Thinking about the length of the punch card, the top and bottom need to match up so that when the card rolls through, the pattern will continue seamlessly. The same is true of the edges of the card because the pattern will repeat widthways too. You can see how this works in the picture here of a punch card that I have put into repeat as an example.

I find the edges of the design trickier to match up than the top and bottom, so I always start on graph paper, mapping out more than one repeat of the design, then move the design onto the punch card. There are many free resources available online where you can download knitting graph paper in the right ratios for your project; this is another reason why it's a good idea to have a tension swatch using your yarns and an existing punch card before you start designing.

Another thing you need to be aware of when designing your pattern is floats. These are the pieces of yarn that travel across the back of the knitted fabric, and you don't want them to be too long. What this means for your design is that you should try to avoid having large areas where there is no detail or pattern. As a general rule, I try to have no floats bigger than eight to ten stitches, depending on the tension of the fabric I am working on. If you have some large motifs and you want large spaces between them, a background pattern of single stitches can be a really effective way to catch the floats.

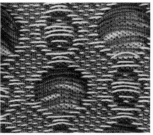

A punch-card pattern with single stitches to catch the floats.

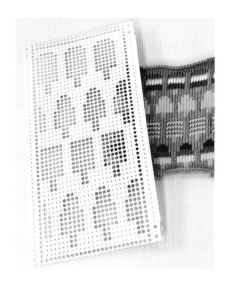

Ice lolly punch card and multicoloured knitted fabric.

If you want to change the colour in your design partway through, making a three- (or more) colour design, this colour change can only happen across a full row, so you need to plan that into your design. Remember, you can only ever use two colours at any one time when knitting with a punch card. I love to use the two-colour punch-card method and change yarns to add more colours to the fabric, which is a very easy way to make really interesting designs.

If you are working with text or a motif that you want to face a certain way, bear in mind that the knitted fabric is mirrored from what you see on the punch card when it is in the machine. Therefore you will need to either write text backwards on the punch card or cheat by drawing it out on the back of the card before punching it out. This is the same for motifs.

GARMENT TECHNIQUES

Before we can use punch cards to create a garment in this chapter's project, there are some more techniques that need to be covered. These include creating a hem on your knitted fabric, construction using the knitting machine, and how to knit a neck band for a garment. These are all done using the main bed of your knitting machine.

Lifted Hems

Creating a lifted hem is a simple technique that gives a neat, finished edge to your knitting. Not only does it stop the bottom of the fabric from rolling up, but if you make the mock rib version, it also gives the look of a rib edge to your fabric without using a ribber bed. I will go through both types here.

The first thing to think about for this technique is waste yarn, as it will be needed for the cast-on. We used it when removing the knitting from the machine on waste in Chapter 2, and looked at

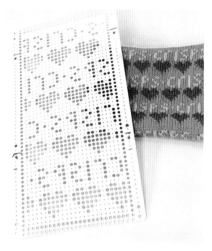

Text designed into a punch card along with motifs, and the resulting knitted fabric.

DESIGNING YOUR OWN PUNCH CARD
1. Knit a tension swatch using the correct yarns and an existing punch card.
2. Sketch out your design onto graph paper, making sure the edges and top and bottom match up.
3. Draw the design onto the punch card, mirroring the design if text or directional motifs are used.
4. Punch out the holes.
5. Feed into the machine and knit your design.

Solid lifted hem knitted in two colours.

Mock rib lifted hem in one-by-one layout.

how we could use this method without actually wasting yarn by unravelling the waste and keeping it to reuse.

It is best to use a waste yarn that is smooth and a contrasting colour to the lifted hem you will be creating. You will also need a yarn for the lifted hem, and a second contrasting yarn for the remainder of the swatch. For this technique you will also need a single-end transfer tool.

Solid Lifted Hem

For my swatch, I knitted over forty needles and knitted twenty rows in waste yarn. You might knit more or fewer rows depending on the thickness of your yarn, but you need enough to hold onto for when you lift the hem.

1. Using your waste yarn and the quick cast-on method, knit over any number of needles you like for this swatch.
2. Swap from waste yarn to the yarn you want to use for the lifted hem.
3. Before you knit across with this yarn, increase the stitch size by one whole number. This is so that you have a loose row of stitches to pick up when you lift the hem.
4. Knit your first row in the hem yarn at this larger stitch size.
5. Change your dial to the standard stitch size for your yarn and continue to knit as many rows as you like for half of the lifted hem; this will be the full height of the hem once it has been lifted.
6. Increase the stitch size by half a number or two clicks, and knit a loose row; this helps the hem to fold in the centre and stay folded.

7. Return to the original stitch size and knit the same number of rows as you knitted before the loose row.
9. Remove the comb and weights.
10. Using your transfer tool, find the second stitch from the end; start here because it is easier to find than the first stitch. When you have found the stitch, pick it up and place it on the second needle.
11. Do the same thing with the third and fourth stitches to secure the bottom of the fabric to the machine.
12. Find the first stitch. It is often quite tight and you might need to ease it out a little to lift it onto the first needle at the edge you started at.
13. Once you have that edge secured and are happy that stitches one to four are on the correct needles, keep going all the way across the fabric until all the stitches have been lifted and are on the needles in working position.
14. Your lifted hem is complete and you are ready to continue knitting your sample. Before you knit across, push all the needles up into their top position to move both the active and lifted stitches down onto the stem of the needle.
15. Remove the waste yarn to avoid the possibility of it getting caught under the carriage as you knit across. Simply unravel the waste from the bottom to keep it all in one piece; you will just have to pull the end through on the edges as you go.
16. Swap to the yarn you are knitting with for the main part of your sample if it is different (in my example here, I used a contrast hem).
17. Reattach your comb and weights before knitting the rest of the fabric.

Creating a solid lifted hem. The waste yarn is knitted first.

Half the hem knitted.

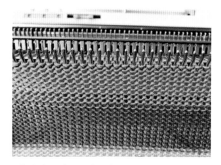
Whole hem knitted and ready to lift onto the machine needles.

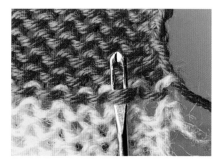
The second stitch from the end of the knitting.

Placing the second stitch onto the needle.

Lifting the first stitch at the edge of the fabric.

All stitches lifted and needles in top position.

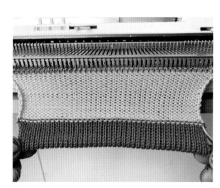
Lifted hem and fabric knitted.

RAVEL CORD

If you have a ravel cord, you can knit this in as the last row of the waste yarn section, as this helps to separate the waste from the hem knitting more clearly and makes removing the waste yarn easier – you just pull the ravel cord out.

Mock Rib Lifted Hem

To create a lifted hem in a one-by-one mock rib pattern, follow the same stages as above, but start in the required rib layout and lift stitches onto empty needles to avoid holes.

1. For a one-by-one mock rib hem, use the quick cast-on method, casting on to every other needle, and don't bring the rest of the needles up into working position.

2. Follow the same process as for the solid hem until you are at the point where you have knitted the loose row and one knitted row of your hem (step 4).

3. At this point, we need to consider the stitch size; because this area of your knitting has ladders in it, you will want to knit it tighter than when knitting the main fabric. This is usually a few numbers below your usual stitch size, but will depend on the yarn you are using.

4. From here, knit the hem in the same way you did for the solid lifted hem, with a looser row at the centre, where it will fold.

5. When you have knitted the required rows and are ready to lift the hem, push all the empty needles up into working position

6. Lift the first row of the hem up onto the empty needles; you lift onto these rather than the needles with stitches on to prevent holes from forming at the beginning of the solid knitted area.

7. Your mock rib lifted hem is complete, and you are ready to continue into knitting your sample. Before you knit across, push all the needles up as far as they will go, to move both the active and lifted stitches down onto the stem of the needle.

8. Remove the waste yarn to avoid the possibility of it getting caught under the carriage as you knit across. Simply unravel the waste from the bottom to keep it all in one piece; you will just have to pull the end through on the edges as you go.

9. Swap to the yarn you are knitting with for the main part of your sample if it is different to the hem yarn.

10. Reattach your comb and weights before knitting the rest of the fabric.

For a mock rib lifted hem, start with the waste yarn as before. Here the loose row at the start of the lifted hem has been knitted.

Half of the mock rib hem knitted.

Needles pushed into working position.

Stitches lifted onto the empty needles.

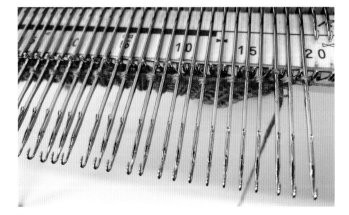

Needles pushed up into top position.

Alternatively, if you want to create a two-by-one mock rib lifted hem, simply start in a two in, one out needle layout.

When lifting the stitches, again work one stitch over, placing knitted stitches onto the empty needles to provide a solid row of stitches to start your main knitting on. If you lift stitches directly onto stitches and leave the empty needles empty, new stitches will need to form on the first knitted row and this will not have a solid appearance.

For any mock rib hem, you can also cast on as you do for a solid hem and transfer into your rib layout on the row after the first loose row. This gives you a full solid row of stitches to lift onto the needles at the end of the knitted hem.

Mock rib lifted hem using a two-by-one layout.

TOP TIP

When you are well practised at lifted hems, you can use a multiple-end tool to lift a number of stitches at once, making the process much quicker. Try a two-prong tool and work up from there.

Lifted Hem Effects

The hem of a garment can be a good place to add some interest through colour or stitch effects. Something as simple as adding a stripe to the hem design or making it half one colour and half another can make the finish of the garment feel really special. These adjustments are usually more effective on solid hems but some, such as stripes, can also work very well on a mock rib hem. More information about how these are created can be found in Chapter 7.

Tipped hem. Adding a stripe in the centre of the lifted hem gives a small amount of colour on the edge.

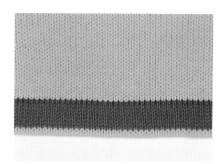

Half-and-half knitted hem, creating a secret little contrast colour inside the garment.

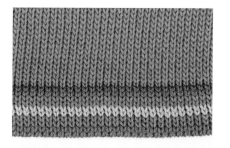

Striped lifted hem to add interest to the design.

Picot lifted hem created by transferring out every third stitch on the centre row and leaving the needles in working position.

CONSTRUCTION

The project at the end of this chapter takes you through knitting a garment. As well as knitting panels for it, you will need to join the knitted pieces together; this process is often referred to as linking. You have already learned all the skills you need to do this and will just be using them in a slightly different way to link pieces together. Follow the instructions in this section to practise linking swatches together.

We have looked at lifting live stitches up onto working needles to create a lifted hem. This technique of hanging live stitches onto the machine needles is used to create seams in all sorts of projects; edge stitches can be rehung onto the machine to create seams in a similar way.

The other technique that is used for linking on the machine is the latch tool cast-off, so if you didn't practise this when learning to cast off, try it now before trying these construction techniques.

Rehanging Live Stitches

When you remove knitted pieces on waste yarn, you will be left with a row of live stitches – the stitches on the last knitted row in your main knitted piece. In garment panels, these will usually be at the shoulders, top of the sleeves and in the neck line.

To practise this seaming technique, knit two swatches, forty stitches wide and forty rows long in any yarn with the last row knitted at a loose stitch size, followed by fifteen rows in waste yarn.

Knitted swatches to practise linking.

1. Take one swatch and hang the loose row of live stitches onto empty needles with the front of the fabric facing you.

2. Take the second piece and hang the loose row of live stitches onto the same needles with the back of the fabric facing you.

3. If you are joining all the stitches in your piece of fabric, you can remove the waste at this stage. If you are joining the shoulder seam of a piece with no neck shaping, you will leave the waste yarn on until both shoulder seams and the neckline have been joined.

4. Optional step: push all needles into hold position and knit across to join the pieces and give a single loop to work with.

5. Cast off using the latch tool cast-off method, then remove from the machine.

6. Gently press the seam using a steam iron to help it lie flat before moving on to any more linking.

TOP TIP

When working with live stitches, it is essential that you hang every stitch onto a needle and don't miss any out; if you miss one, this stitch will drop when the waste is removed.

Rehanging Edge Stitches

This is different from hanging live stitches because these are closed stitches, the fabric isn't as flexible and the tension is different. When you do this, you are hanging knitted rows rather than stitches, and you will have more rows per centimetre than stitches per centimetre. If you tried to hook up all the stitches at the edge of a swatch it would get very tight and you wouldn't be able to work with it. A good rule of thumb is to lift two in every three, or three in every four stitches onto the machine needles.

Also, unlike with live stitches, when hanging the edge stitches, we work one row in from the edge rather than hanging the very edge stitch. For this process, you don't need to knit a separate swatch, as you can use the swatches that you have just joined at the top.

1. Take the first swatch and hang it onto the machine with the front of the fabric facing you, working one full row of stitches in from the edge of the fabric.

2. Take the second swatch and hang it at the centre and the far end of the piece to start with; this will help you to hang the rest of the stitches evenly. Then hang the remaining stitches.

3. Optional step: push all needles into hold position and knit across to join the pieces and give a single loop to work with.

4. Join these two pieces using the latch tool cast-off method and remove from the machine.

5. Gently press the seam using a steam iron to help it lie flat before moving on to any more linking.

TOP TIP

When working with edge stitches on the second piece of fabric, I find it helpful to pull the needles on the machine up through the stitches so the fabrics are both sitting on the shaft of the needle.

Hand Linking

If you find hooking the knitting back onto your machine very fiddly, or you are just really good at doing things by hand, you might prefer hand linking. To do this, it is best to use a latch tool, as this gives you the same kind of seam you get through using a linking machine or linking on the knitting machine. Because you are working by hand, it is best to pin the pieces together before starting to join them.

As with linking on the machine, make sure you steam each seam after you have completed it.

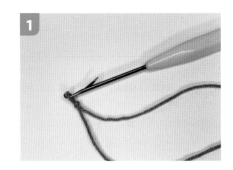

1. To start, make a slipknot and place it onto the hook of your latch tool.

2. Pass the latch tool through both of your fabrics, working one stitch from the edge.

3. The slipknot will slide down the latch tool, opening the latch.

4. With the yarn at the back of your work, place the yarn into the hook of the latch tool.

5. Pull the tool towards you, pulling the yarn through the existing loop and creating a new stitch.

6. Continue in this way, passing the tool through the fabric and pulling yarn through to stitch the two layers together.

7. When you get to the end of your seam, simply cut the yarn and pull it through the last stitch on your tool.

Constructing a Garment

Now we have looked at linking both live and edge stitches, we will consider how these skills would be applied to a project. You can link seams for any project using these methods, but before tackling your first garment, let us look at how this would be put together.

Due to the way that the neck band and sleeves are attached, there is a specific order to follow when linking knitted garment panels:

1. Front and back panel linked at one shoulder
2. Neck band knitted and attached
3. Front and back panels linked at second shoulder
4. Sleeve head linked to arm hole on both sides
5. Side seam and sleeve seam on both sides

With this in mind, before you can knit and construct a garment with all the necessary trims, we need to look at how to knit and attach a neck band.

Neck Band

As well as creating mock rib trims in a garment, when working on a single-bed machine you can also knit a mock rib neck band to finish the neck off neatly. Again, this uses techniques you have already learned, but applying them in a different way.

When you get to this stage, you will have already knitted the hems on the garment panels. You can either work to the same height as these, knitting the same number of rows for the hems and the neck band, or alter the number of rows slightly if required.

Before knitting the neck band, as well as the height, you need to work out the number of needles to knit it over. To do this, you first need to knit the front and back panels of your garment then complete these steps:

1. Mark the neck opening width onto the panels using pins.
2. Join one shoulder seam (see the project at the end of this chapter).
3. Count the number of live stitches in the neck area for you to link the neck band onto; **or**, if shaping has been used, hang the neck area onto the machine to find the number of stitches you will need to knit this over.

Finished garment with a mock rib knitted neck band.

The project at the end of this chapter does not involve shaping, therefore the panels will be removed on waste yarn, leaving live stitches that you can count. However, when a shaped neckline has been knitted, you would rehang the neck area onto the machine to see how many needles you will need to knit the neck band over.

When you know the number of needles, you will knit the neck band in the same way you did for the mock rib lifted hem, as follows:

1. Cast on over the required number of needles for the mock rib neck band using waste yarn.
2. Knit a loose row to start with; these stitches will be lifted.
3. Knit the remainder of the neck band with a loose row in the middle.
4. Lift all the stitches onto the relevant needles.

When the mock rib has been lifted, you can knit one row before hanging the jumper onto the machine to attach the neck. This reduces the number of loops you will be working with when you link these pieces together. To do this, push all the needles up into hold position so the stitches travel down the needles, and knit across to join the mock rib together. At this point, you can remove the waste yarn and ravel cord (if used).

When you have garment panels knitted, you will hang these back onto the needles that you have knitted the neck band on, and use the latch tool cast-off method to join the garment panel to the neck band. We will go through this in more detail in the project.

Neck Band Knitting and Linking Practice

Before you do this on your garment, have a go at knitting a swatch, then a mock rib neck band to match its width, and joining them on your machine.

Start by knitting a swatch ending with a loose row, and remove this from the machine on waste yarn. Then follow the steps in the photo sequence.

1. Cast on over the correct number of needles in mock rib setting, knit the neck band to the required height and lift stitches onto the empty needles.

2. Join the neck band by knitting one row. Remove waste from the neck band so it's ready to attach to the knitted swatch.

3. Hang the swatch onto the needles with the reverse of the fabric facing you; this would be the neck opening on a garment.

4. Link the swatch and the neck band together using the latch tool cast-off method, then remove it from the machine.

You can see how neat the finish is when you add a neck band to the top of a swatch: imagine how good this will look on your first knitted garment!

MEASUREMENTS

Another thing to understand before making your first garment are the measurements you need for knitted garments. These will vary, depending on what you are making. To start with, we are focusing on a top with no shaping and short sleeves. If you want to include shaping, you will need to consider this in your measurements too (*see* Chapter 7).

The great thing about knitting the fabric for your own clothes is that you can make each piece the exact right size for you. When planning a garment, I use measurements from existing garments whose fit and style I like. If you have a garment that you know works for your body shape or is a length that you really like, then it makes sense to use that as a guide. Sometimes I take the measurement of a sleeve from one garment and a body length from a different one.

Mock rib neck band attached to a straight fabric swatch.

To measure an existing garment, follow where the measurement lines are on the garment diagram shown here, and the guide below, making a note of each measurement. I like to sketch out a simple garment shape to note the measurements down on.

Illustration of a knitted top with arrows
showing the measurements that are needed.

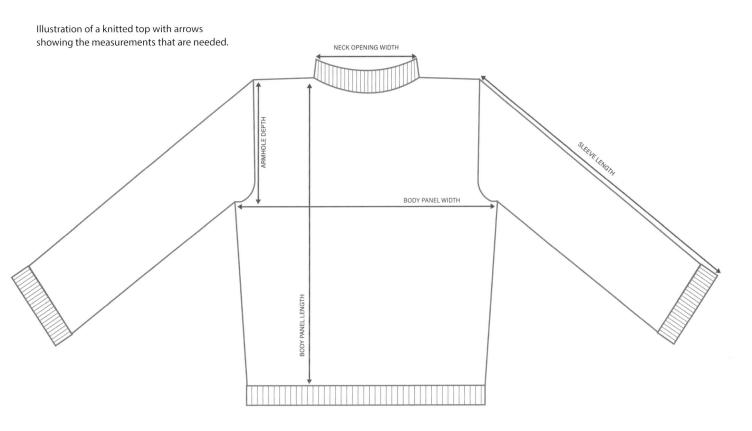

Body panel width
Measure across the garment from armpit to armpit.

Body panel length
Measure from the top of the shoulder down to the bottom of the garment.

Armhole depth
Measure from the armpit to the top of the sleeve area.

Sleeve length
Measure from the top of the sleeve to the end of the sleeve.

Neck opening width
Measure across the neck opening in the garment.

We will look at how these measurements translate into measurements for knitted panels when we come to plan the panels. Garment panels are covered in more detail in Chapter 7.

GMMRS

Gem in her studio.

Punch cards and pattern swatches.

My name is Gem, and I'm currently based in Norwich, UK. I run a small knitwear brand called GMMRS and I've been machine knitting for eight years.

What brought you to machine knitting and where did you learn?

I found out what machine knitting was though a friend and a textiles course I was doing at the time. I only got a pretty brief tutorial on it, as the institution wasn't really encouraging or equipped for knitters so I found myself having to pursue it more on my own; but when I found a machine on eBay for a bargain, I bought it on a whim and basically fell in love. I became mostly self-taught through books and YouTube. There's a great number of resources out there that you can find from a little digging around! Not to mention a great community of machine knitters on places like Instagram with tips and tricks too.

Can you tell us about the knitting machines you use now and why they are the right machines for your practice?

I use a single-bed Knitmaster 260, which is a domestic knit machine from the 1970s. It's a pretty standard machine with manual controls and carriage with punch-card capabilities. It was my first-ever machine and for eight years now it's still the main one I use because of its ease.

I just love that such a simple machine can produce endless patterns, textures and garments with a little imagination. It's always nice hearing that people are surprised when I tell them I use such a simple machine compared to the detailed knits I can make from it.

How about your design process – what inspires you?

I love to explore the bright, bold and borderline garish patterns of the 1980s and 90s – I definitely take a lot of inspirations from the fashion, decor and media of that time. I'm a design maximalist and keep a big log of all patterns, shapes and colours I love whenever I see them!

When you've got your inspiration, how do you take it from idea to the finished product?

Sketching and sampling! Knitting isn't the quickest process, so it's best to try to anticipate your outcome before starting so you don't end up hating it and having to unravel a whole piece. For designing, it's definitely worth looking into getting some sort of digital tablet and pencil. I spent years scribbling in sketchbooks with half-working felt-tip pens until I discovered digital devices. You can expand your ideas so quickly and sketch up to ten different colour ways in minutes.

Do you have any favourite yarns that you like to work with?
Anything four-ply is my ideal yarn! It knits up the perfect density to be wearable nearly all year round. I love eco cotton or a cotton/poly blend as they steam so smoothly and wash and wear well too. It's also important to be aware of the environmental impact of yarns and materials, so, if you can, try to favour small businesses that are transparent with their environmental origins and production chains.

This chapter has been all about using pattern and colour; can you tell us a bit about how you use punch-card patterns and colour in your work?
I use punch cards in pretty much everything I knit as they're super versatile and can be used in so many different ways. I use Fair Isle more than anything, which allows multicolour patterned knit, so I use it to make motifs and repeat patterns mainly. I also use punch cards to create textured knitting on some of my plainer knits by using settings like tuck or slip stitch to make a thinner lace-style knit or an even chunkier bubbly knit.

Do you have any tips on designing your own punch cards?
Definitely expect some trial and error, and get yourself some gridded paper for practice. Fitting an entire pattern into the standard twenty-four stitches across seems daunting, but that's part of the fun of being creative and is so rewarding when finished. Remember to pattern match each side if trying to make a repeat so you're left with seamless design, and be cautious of long floats on the back of your knits if using a single bed with no jacquard settings.

How about choosing colours for a project – where do you start?
I'm a sucker for using lots of different bright colours in my knits at once. I usually start by making colour and pattern swatches and see how shades knit up next to each other. One of the pros of colour swatches is that if you don't like the outcome they can be unravelled easily and the yarn reused. I sometimes save mine and reuse them for fun scrap jumpers when I have enough lying around. I definitely think that taking risks with colours pays off and that you'll be surprised that most actually look great together: experiment and mix together shades you love, and just go for it!

Do you have any general advice for people who are learning to use a knitting machine? Is there anything you wish you had known when you were starting out?
That it will 100 per cent get easier with perseverance and practice. It personally took me years to finally become confident enough to knit garments easily and quickly. My advice is to keep at it. The first

A range of swatches that have been knitted using punch cards.

Garments created using punch cards.

little while when learning can be frustrating and intimidating but don't be tempted to give up. Go at your own pace and you will pick up more and more as you go – I'm eight years into machine knitting and I still learn new things all the time. Also, it's super important to oil and clean your machine and carriage of dust regularly to keep it singing and knitting happily.

Where can people find your work?
🌐 gmmrs.com
📷 @gmmrs

Sweet and Simple Block Jumper

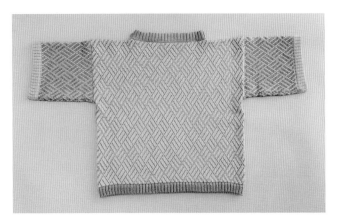

Finished knitted top using a punch-card design and mock rib lifted hems.

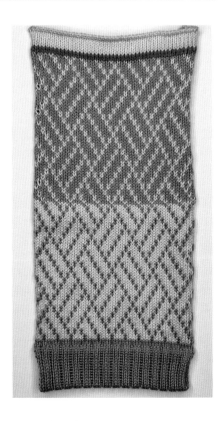

Tension swatch of 100 rows knitted over fifty needles in punch card and project yarns with a mock rib lifted hem.

For the second project we are jumping into making a garment; it might seem a big step to go from a scarf to a top but we are keeping it very simple. This top is made up of four rectangles, which gives a boxy fit, and a high slash neck. I find this shape comfortable and easy to wear with lots of different outfits. I usually go for a short sleeve with this kind of shape because it has a wide opening, but you can make the sleeves any length you like.

In this project, you will also be using a punch card to create a patterned fabric all over the top. The punch card I used is one that came with my Brother knitting machine; if you don't have this card, you can use a similar one, or, if you really like the design, you can punch it out yourself. As with the scarf, you will make a tension swatch, then calculate all your own values for knitting the project. This allows you to make a garment that is right for you and is great practice for when you get to designing your own knits from scratch.

Before you make the tension swatch, you need to select your yarns; I have used four-ply soft cotton yarns. As you can see from the picture, I have used two colours and swapped the main and contrast on the sleeves and body as well as changing the trim colours. If you want a less busy look, you could use the same main and contrast colours for the whole garment. In addition to the yarns to knit the top, you will also need a yarn to use for waste knitting.

You will need:

- Yarns to knit the top
- Waste yarn
- Tape measure
- Blocking mats and pins
- Calculator
- Garment/s to measure for fit

TENSION SWATCH

Before we look at the garment measurements, you need a tension swatch. If you have knitted with these yarns using this punch card before, you might know the stitch size you want to use; if not, you will need to knit a swatch using different tensions first, dividing the sections with a contrast colour and recording the stitch sizes used in these.

When you have found the right quality of fabric and the corresponding stitch size, you are ready to knit the main tension swatch. When knitting a garment, I always include a trim in the final tension swatch so that I can use the swatch for both the trim and main fabric calculations. For this garment, I have used a two-by-one mock rib lifted hem and knitted it to the height I would like on the garment by eye. When you knit the rib, make sure you make a note of the number of rows knitted and the tension they were knitted at.

1. Knit your tension swatch, including the mock rib lifted hem.
2. Finish the swatch using the correct method for the yarn you have used.
3. From this tension swatch, find your rows and stitches per cm/inch using the process explained in Chapter 2.
4. Make a note of these values, as you will use them when working out how big each knitted panel will need to be in stitches and rows.
5. Measure the height of your hem on the tension swatch and make a note of how many rows you want to adjust it by, if any; then note down the final values for your mock rib lifted hems.

My values, with a punch card knitted at stitch size 6 using a four-ply soft cotton were 3.2 stitches and four rows per centimetre, and my mock rib hem is 4cm high.

MEASUREMENTS

Because this garment doesn't involve any shaping, we just need to work out how big the body panel and the sleeve panel need to be. To measure an existing garment:

1. Lay out the garment/s you want to measure on a flat surface.
2. Take the following measurements from the body of the garment and make a note of each: body width, body length, neck opening width.
3. Take the following measurements from the sleeve of the garment and make a note of each: armhole depth, sleeve length.

To transfer these garment measurements to panel measurements, it is helpful to draw out each panel. The only measurement that is adjusted from garment to panel is the armhole depth, which is multiplied by two to give the value for the width of the sleeve panel.

At this stage, you also need to take into account how deep you want the rib trims to be on the garment. I put the full panel length measurement on one side and the rib trim to body split on the other side.

Body panel measurements
Body panel width, body panel length, neck opening width

Sleeve panel measurements
Sleeve panel width (armhole depth × 2), sleeve panel length

These are my body and sleeve panel sketches with the width and length measurements in centimetres. You can see the length measurements have been split into mock rib and main sections.

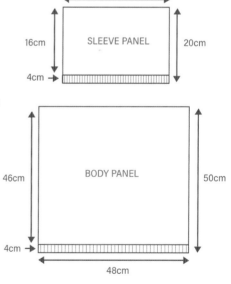

SLEEVE PANEL
38cm
16cm
20cm
4cm

BODY PANEL
46cm
50cm
4cm
48cm

Calculations

Now you have got the measurements for your body and sleeve panels, these need to be transferred from cm/inches into stitches and rows. To do this, simply use the values from your tension swatch and multiply these by the measurements of your panels. My tension is 3.2 stitches and four rows per centimetre. Below are my panel calculations. Follow the same process with your own tension values and measurements to work out the stitches and rows needed for each panel.

Example panel calculations:

Body panel
Width = 3.2 sts × 48cm = 153.6 (round up to 154 stitches)
Length = 4 rows × 46cm = 184 rows

Sleeve panel
Width = 3.2 sts × 38cm = 128 stitches
Length = 4 rows × 16cm = 64 rows

Now you have all the values you need for the mock rib lifted hems and the panels, you are ready to start knitting.

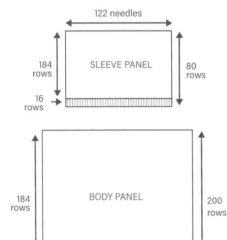

122 needles

184 rows   SLEEVE PANEL   80 rows

16 rows

These are my panel sketches labelled with the width and length in stitches and knitted rows.

184 rows   BODY PANEL   200 rows

16 rows

154 needles

KNITTING THE PANELS

As with the scarf project, the first stage is to make a knitting list for each panel. You will be knitting two body panels and two sleeve panels. On my top, I knitted the trim so that it contrasts with the dominant colour in the punch card pattern; whichever colours you are using for the trims and main panels, make a note of this on the knitting list.

Use the format below to help with your own knitting process. The panels are removed from the machine on waste yarn.

Panel knitting steps:

1. Cast on over _____ needles in desired rib layout using waste yarn, knit ten rows.
2. Change to the hem yarn, knit one loose row then zero the row counter.
3. Change stitch size to mock rib stitch size _____ and knit one row.
4. Knit _____ rows followed by one slack row, then another _____ rows at the rib tension.
5. Lift the mock rib hem back onto the needles and push all needles up into hold position.
6. Change stitch size to main fabric quality _____.
7. Feed in the punch card and change the machine to the correct settings to knit this.
8. Change the yarn to the pattern colour for punch-card knitting and knit set-up row for the punch card.
9. Zero the row counter.
10. Add your second yarn for the punch-card pattern and knit _____ rows to the top of the panel.
11. Disengage the punch card and knit one row in the dominant colour at slack tension.
12. Change to waste yarn, knit fourteen rows and remove the panel from the machine.

When you have written out your knitting list for the body panel, follow it to knit two of these. Do the same for the sleeve panels, writing out the list then following it to knit each panel. You will now have four panels and are almost ready to put the top together. Give all the panels a gentle steam at this stage to make them easier to work with.

Body panel and sleeve panel with lifted hem and waste knitted.

Neck opening marked with pins.

NECK BAND

The last thing you will knit is the neck band. It is knitted in the same way as a lifted hem, but first you need to work out how big you want it to be.

Neck Opening

Before you can work out how many needles you want to knit it over, you need to decide how big you want the neck opening to be. If you have a slash-neck top whose neck-opening size you like, then measure that; if not, measure another neck opening on an existing garment at the widest point. The neck opening width on my top is 24cm, making the whole neck opening 48cm all the way round. Now you are ready to mark the neck area on the panels.

1. Pin the panels at the shoulders, leaving the neck area open, and slip it on over your head to check it goes on all right. If it is a bit tight then widen it, or narrow it if it feels too wide and loose.
2. When you are happy with the width of the neck opening, mark this on both the front and back panel separately using pins; do this by measuring half of the neck width out from

the centre of the panel and placing a pin vertically next to the edge stitch of the neck opening.
3. Check that you have the same number of stitches on each side of the pins. This section will be the shoulder.
4. Do this on both the front and back panels. All of my pins are sitting forty stitches in from the edge, making the shoulder area forty stitches wide.

JOINING THE FIRST SHOULDER

When you have this marked out and have checked the number of stitches in the shoulder areas, you are ready to link the first shoulder to prepare for linking the neck band onto the top.

1. Hang one shoulder segment of the front and back panels onto the machine with right sides facing, using the stitches in the last slack row of the body panel to hang them onto the machine.
2. Link the first shoulder seam using the latch tool cast-off method and the same colour yarn as the stitches.
3. When you take this off the machine, you have one shoulder seam linked and are ready to work out how many needles you will knit the neck band over.

Shoulder area of one panel hung onto the machine.

Shoulder area of both panels hung onto the machine ready to link.

Working in this way, it is important to leave the waste yarn on the garment until the construction is complete and neck band attached. Gently press the shoulder seam at this point.

CALCULATING NECK BAND WIDTH

Because the panel has been removed using waste yarn, the live stitches at the top of the panel will be linked directly onto the neck band.

With this in mind, to work out how many needles to knit the neck band over, you simply count the number of stitches over the whole neck area, from the pin to the shoulder seam – you should have the same number of stitches on the front and back panels and need to count all of these.

My neck band area is 148 stitches in total, 74 on the front panel and 74 on the back panel.

KNITTING AND ATTACHING THE NECK BAND

Now you know over how many needles you need to knit your neck band, you can follow the neck band knitting instructions below:

1. Cast on in waste yarn in your desired rib layout over the number of needles required.
2. Knit the required number of rows in the yarn you have chosen for the neck band, remembering to knit the slack rows at the start and mid-point of the neck band.
3. Lift the stitches over the whole width of the neck band onto the machine needles to complete the mock rib neck band.
4. When this is complete, you are ready to join the band to the neck of the garment.

Back body panel hung onto the knitted mock rib neck band.

Neck band stitches lifted onto the knitting machine.

5. Starting with the back of the garment at the right-hand side of the machine, hang the body panel stitches in the neck area onto the needles with the right sides together. The shoulder seam should line up with the zero on the machine.

6. Continue lifting the stitches until all the live stitches from the neck band area are hung on to the needles with the neck band on them.

7. When this is done, use the latch tool cast-off method to join the body panels to the neck band.

8. When the last stitch has been secured, lift it off the machine.

9. Before joining the second shoulder, steam the neck band area to help it to lie flat.

JOINING THE SECOND SHOULDER

When you join the second shoulder, you will also join the seam of the neck band in the same way.

1. Lift the second section of shoulder stitches onto the machine in the same way you did with the first.

2. When you get to the neck band, lift the outside layer of the mock rib neck band, working one stitch width from the edge of the knitting.

3. When all the shoulder and neck band stitches have been lifted onto the machine, push all the needles up into hold position.

4. Use the latch tool cast-off method to join this seam.

5. Take the pieces off the machine, remove the waste yarn and press the shoulder seams.

ATTACHING THE SLEEVES

Now you have the front and back panels joined together, you are ready to attach the sleeves. Because we took the sleeves off on waste yarn, you have live stitches at the top of these panels that you will be using to link them to the body panels.

Here, we are linking live stitches to edge panel stitches, so for the body panel, rather than counting stitches, you will use the armhole depth measurement; this is the initial measurement you took before translating it into the sleeve panel width. Simply measure the armhole depth from the shoulder seam down the body panel and mark with a pin where you want the underarm of the garment to be.

The depth of the armhole is half the full width of the sleeve panel – 20cm in my case, so I simply measured 20cm down from the shoulder seam and placed a pin here on both the front and back of the garment. This is so that I know where to start and finish hanging the body panel to connect it to the sleeve panel. The shoulder seam will be the mid-point and will sit at the zero when hung onto the machine.

1. Centring over the zero, bring the same number of needles you knitted the sleeve panel on up into working position.
2. With the right side facing you, hang the body panel onto the needles, with the shoulder seam at the zero.
3. To help hang the stitches evenly, hang a few edge stitches and the central stitches first.
4. Then hang a few stitches in the centre of each of the body panel areas before lifting the rest of the stitches onto the empty needles.
5. Remember, when hanging stitches at the edge of a fabric, always work one full stitch in from the edge of the fabric to keep it nice and even.
6. When all the body panel stitches in the sleeve area have been hung onto the machine, you can hang the sleeve panel onto the same needles before joining them.
7. Because the sleeve has live stitches, you can just work from one side to the other, hanging a stitch on every needle.
8. At this point, you can remove the waste from the top of the sleeve panel, link these together using the latch tool cast-off method, then take it off the machine.
9. Follow steps 1 to 8 for the second sleeve.
10. Once you have finished both sleeves, press the shoulder seams.

Now you have the shoulder seams joined, the neck band linked on and the sleeves joined to the body panels.

Body panel hung onto the machine at the edges, shoulder seam and body panel areas.

Sleeve hung onto the same needles as the body panel.

JOINING SLEEVE AND SIDE SEAMS

This last seam on each side will join the sides and sleeves together, and you will include the hems as you did when joining the neck band. Work with the front of the fabrics facing each other, and remember to hang the stitches evenly.

1. Place the underarm seam over the zero to start with, and hook up the ends and centres of each panel onto the needles in preparation for lifting the rest.
2. Lift the remaining stitches onto the empty needles, lifting onto two needles for every three row stitches to keep it even. You will end up with one whole edge, from the sleeve hem to the bottom of the body hem, hung onto the machine, with the front of the fabric facing you.

3. Hang the stitches from the other half of the garment onto the same needles; start by hanging the underarm seam and trims to match up with what you already have hung on the machine. Remember to hang the centres and a few other points in the panels before lifting the rest of the stitches.
4. When all the stitches are hung on the machine, use the latch tool cast-off method to join the panels.
5. When the seam is complete, remove the panels from the machine then repeat the same steps on the other side of the top.
6. Remove it from the machine, work in any loose ends and give the seams a press so they lie flat. After this, you can wash or steam and block the garment depending on the yarn you have used and what it needs in terms of finishing. Then enjoy wearing it...hopefully for many years!

One side of the jumper hung onto the needles at several points.

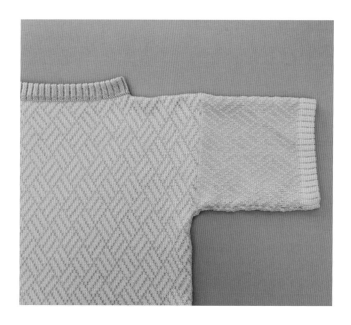

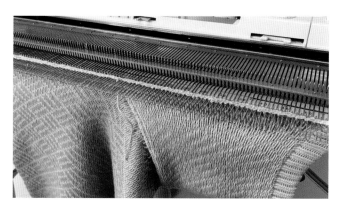

Both parts hung on the machine ready to seam up the side and sleeve of the garment.

CHAPTER 4

SIMPLE SHAPING

One of the many wonderful things about knitwear is that you can shape the pieces as you knit them, which means there is very little waste. In this chapter we are going to look at different ways to shape knitting. Shaping is a really simple skill that people can often be intimidated by; just remember – if you can use a transfer tool, you can shape a fabric.

INCREASING

Increasing is simply adding stitches to the knitting area, either one needle at a time or in groups of needles. There are also different methods you can use that to create different effects in the fabric.

Single-Needle Increase

This increase involves adding a single needle to the edge of the knitting to gradually widen the knitting area. It is a very simple process but, as you can see from the photo, the increase is visible, so you would usually use this method when the selvedge will be hidden in a seam.

To carry out this increase, push the empty needle up into working position on the same side as the carriage, then knit across. The yarn will lie into this needle, then form a knitted stitch on the next row.

To make the increase even on both sides, you will then have to push the needle at the opposite side (where your carriage is now sitting) up into working position and knit across.

Single-needle selvedge increase at both sides.

Needle pushed up.

Yarn laid into the needle hook.

Increase on both sides of knitting.

You have now increased the width of your knitting area by two stitches over two knitted rows. You can carry on with this pattern to practise increasing and make a sample; when shaping, you will often knit a number of rows between the increase rows, depending on the angle you want to create.

Transfer Increase

This increase still only adds a single needle at the edge, but it gives a smoother edge to the knitted fabric, because rather than new stitches being formed at the edge of the fabric, existing stitches are moved over to widen it. This method also allows you to make an increase at both edges in the same row, which makes shaping calculations easier and results in a more even fabric.

You can see that when using this technique, holes are created by transferring the stitches. On the right-hand side of the fabric, the holes have been left open and on the left-hand side they have been closed to show the difference. It is up to you whether you want to close them or leave them open for decoration.

With this increase, you can choose how many stitches you transfer depending on how you want the edge to look. The more stitches you move over by one position, the further into the fabric this shaping will be visible.

Before you have a go at this, choose which transfer tool you want to try; in the example shown here, I am using the two-pronged transfer tool to move two stitches at a time. Simply move two stitches at the edge of your knitting over by one position.

If you want to close the hole, use a single-end tool to lift the bump of the stitch directly under the stitch next to the empty needle and lift it onto the needle to close the hole.

Do this at both edges of the knitting to increase by two stitches in one row, then just knit across to continue working your sample. You can increase as frequently as you like using this technique. If you are new to this, I suggest you knit samples using single-, double- and triple-ended tools to see the different effect you get at the edge of the fabric.

Transfer increase using a triple-ended transfer tool with holes left on the right-hand side.

Transfer increases using, from left to right, single-, double-, and triple-ended transfer tools.

Moving two stitches one position to the right.

Identifying the stitch to lift.

Lifting this stitch onto the empty needle.

Increasing Multiple Stitches

Sometimes, if you are changing the shape of something dramatically, you might want to increase by a number of stitches at once. To do this, always work on the same side as your carriage because that is where your yarn is. All you need to do is cast on to the needles that you want to add to your knitting area using the e-wrap method. Push the required number of needles up into hold position and wrap the yarn around them as you would for a cast-on.

Knit across once to form stitches on these needles; before you knit back, push the needles back up into hold position so that the stitches can knit without any weight added. Do this every row until you have enough knitting in the new area to hang a weight on.

Extra edge needles pushed up with yarn wrapped round them for multiple-stitch increase.

Extra needles pushed up into hold position before knitting the second row.

Six rows knitted and a weight hung onto the additional fabric.

DECREASING

Decreasing is the process of narrowing a fabric by moving stitches in towards the centre of the knitting area and putting needles out of working position. This is a bit simpler than increasing, but there are still options that can give different effects, depending on how many needles you want to decrease by. If you want to decrease by one or two stitches at each edge, you can use the stitch transfer method, but for any more than that, you will need to close the stitches by casting them off.

If you use the stitch transfer method, the fabric will look different depending on the transfer tool you use. This is because the movement of the stitches can be seen on the surface of the fabric, and the more prongs on the transfer tool, the further into the fabric the visible stitch movement will be.

Stitch transfer decrease, one stitch at a time using a three-pronged tool.

Closed stitch decrease, taking groups of five needles out every two rows.

If you use a three-pronged tool, for example, simply pick up the three stitches at the edge of the fabric and move them in by one position. Do the same at the other edge if you are narrowing the fabric at both sides. When you have done this, remember to put the empty needles at the edges of the knitting area out of working position.

Another option is to create a fully fashioned decrease. This involves one more step than the transfer decrease, but gives a slightly smoother finish on the front of the fabric. To do this, empty the needle next to the stitches you are going to transfer before moving them over by one position. It doesn't matter how many stitches you are moving – you just need to empty the needle that the innermost stitch of your decrease will be moving onto.

When decreasing, the fabric narrows and the edges can become tight. To avoid this and keep an even take-down tension, simply hang the weights directly into the fabric close to the top.

You can also decrease by two stitches at each edge by simply using a tool with two or more prongs and moving the stitches by two needle positions. If you want to decrease by more than two stitches, however, you need to cast off the required stitches. You will use the yarn that you have been knitting with to do this, so you always want to cast off at the same side as the carriage. Simply follow the same steps as you would for casting off, then transfer the last new stitch created onto the new edge needle on your knitting. Remember to push the empty needles down into non-working position and lift the cast-off section of fabric off the gate pegs if needed.

If you want to cast off stitches at both edges on the same row, you can use a separate piece of yarn to do this. Simply introduce this yarn after you have transferred the first stitch, using it to make the new stitch as you would with the yarn from the carriage, then use this yarn to cast off the remaining required stitches for this decrease. You will use this technique in underarm shaping, so it is a good one to practise.

From left to right, these decreases have been created using a one-, two- and three-pronged tool.

Three-pronged tool moving three stitches over by one stitch position.

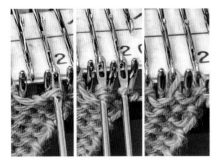

Fully fashioned decrease. Move the stitch next to those you are transferring over to empty the needle, then move the stitches over by one position.

Two-pronged tool moving two stitches over by two stitch positions.

Six stitches cast off and the last stitch placed onto the new edge needle.

PARTIAL KNITTING

As well as adding and removing stitches from the edge of the knitting area to shape your fabric, knitting machines also allow you to create shaping using partial knitting, also known as short-row knitting. This method lets you knit on the exact needles in your knitting area you want to work on, and is great for integral shaping.

Whenever you use the partial knit method, you will always be creating more knitting in one area of your fabric, and this area can be increased or decreased by adjusting needle positions. This approach is often used for neck and shoulder shaping in garments, and for socks.

This technique is straightforward, but there are a few points to keep in mind to help your partial knitting go smoothly and avoid getting holes in the fabric. Firstly, you need to find the hold function on your knitting machine carriage – check your manual for this, as it varies across makes of knitting machine. You then simply push all the needles that you don't want to knit with up into hold position; this is often as high as the needles will go, but check your machine manual for correct positioning. A basic rule of thumb with partial knit is to knit on the side of the fabric closest to the carriage by pushing the needles into the hold position on the opposite side to your carriage.

When you knit across, the needles in hold position will not knit, the yarn simply passing over them. To prevent holes forming where the held stitches meet the knitting, take the yarn under the last needle in hold position; this will be next to the last working needle.

Passing the yarn under the holding needle when knitting just a few rows in one layout is enough to prevent holes, but if you are working a number of rows in the same position, you will want to wrap the yarn around this needle (as you did for the e-wrap cast-on) every few knitted rows to prevent holes forming.

Increasing the Holding Area

To increase the holding area, simply push more needles up into hold position. You can push up as many as you like, but for even shaping you usually add one at a time.

Because there will be more knitting in one part of the fabric than the rest, you will also need to add a weight to the area that is knitting, moving it up as you go to make sure there is enough take-down tension on the stitches for them to knit.

Adding rows over a section of the fabric using partial knitting.

A section of needles pushed up into hold position. One row has been knitted and yarn passed under the edge holding needle to prevent holes from forming.

One needle put into hold position every two knitted rows.

Increasing the Knitting Area

To widen your knitting area, bring needles in hold position back into upper working position. Any needles in this position will be knitted onto when you move the carriage across.

These examples have focused on using shaping on one side of the knitting at a time, which is how you will usually work when using partial knit for shaping garments. Have a go at this to get the hang of it, making wedges at the sides of your fabric. Use a different colour to the main body of your knitted fabric so that you can see the partial knit shaping clearly.

Knitting area increased by needles being returned to upper working position.

Partial Knitting for Sock Shaping

When creating shaping for socks, you will be making a heel and a toe area using partial knitting. This uses the methods of increasing both the knitting and holding areas to create a three-dimensional piece in your otherwise flat knitted sock.

To create the heel and toe, you will be shaping on every knitted row over the desired number of rows for your sock. I have used a contrast colour for the heel here to make the area more visible and clearly separate from the body of the sock. You would follow the exact same process to knit the toe area.

If you want to have a go at this shaping before taking it into a sock, cast on over sixty stitches to mimic the full width of a sock, and knit twenty rows before following the step-by-step instructions to have a go at heel/toe shaping. When you have worked steps 1 to 8, knit another twenty rows before removing the sample from the machine.

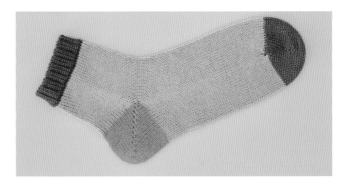

Completed heel and toe areas of a sock that have been shaped using partial knitting.

1. To practise sock shaping, start by putting half the needles into hold position; only the needles knitting the heel are left in working position.

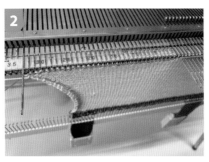

2. Needles at the edge of the knitting area on the opposite side to the carriage are pushed up one at a time, alternating the sides and narrowing the knitting area on every row.

3. To avoid holes when narrowing, remember to pass the yarn under the needle in hold position next to the knitting area.

4. Keep narrowing the knitting area over the next twenty rows to complete half of the heel; this will only differ if using a fine or chunky machine.

5. You are now at the mid-point of the shaping, and from here you will be increasing the knitting width over twenty rows.

6. The edge needle at the same side as the carriage placed into upper working position so it will knit on this row.

7. Continue placing one needle at each edge back into upper working position for twenty rows.

8. All needles on the heel side of the sock are back in working position: you can now move from hold to knitting on all needles.

CALCULATIONS

We have already looked at how to knit and measure a tension swatch to find out your fabric values of stitches and rows/cm or inch; now it is time to look at how to apply these to work out shaping. More detailed and garment-applied versions of this will be covered later in the book, so for now we will concentrate on the basics.

Frequency

Frequency is the term used to describe how often you will be shaping; it also takes into consideration how many stitches you will be adding or removing. Both the tension of your knitted fabric and the kind of shape you want to create will affect this.

To work out the frequency we need to know the following:

- How many needles you are adding or taking away from the knitting
- How many knitted rows you have to add or remove them over

For example, if I have a piece of knitting that is twenty stitches wide and I want to make it thirty stitches wide I need to add ten needles to the knitting area.

I have knitted a tension swatch and calculated that I have twenty knitted rows to widen the knitting over, and will be using the transfer increase method where each increase adds two stitches, one at each side of the fabric.

Using this increase method means that when you are working out how many times you need to increase, you will divide the number of needles you want to add to the fabric by two. For this example, the following is how I would calculate the frequency.

Frequency Calculation Example

Current stitches = 20
Required stitches = 30
Difference in stitches = 10

The difference is the number of needles I will be adding.

Number of needles to add = 10
Number of increases using the transfer increase method =
    number of needles to add ÷ 2
Number of times to increase = 5
Shaping frequency = number of knitted rows to increase over ÷
    number of times to increase:
20 ÷ 5 = 4
Frequency = 4, which means I will increase every fourth row

This example is for increasing; however, for decreasing you still find the difference between the current stitches and the required stitches and calculate the frequency in the same way.

Shaping Calculation Exercise

To practise calculating shaping frequency, let's knit a small shape, one that is widened and then narrowed so that you can practise both increasing and decreasing in the same sample. I swapped colours in the middle so in the photograph you can see where I changed from one to the other.

Knitted shape to practise shaping and learn how to calculate frequency.

Before you start this exercise, make a tension swatch and note down your stitches and rows per cm or inch.

The shape starts at 10cm (4in) and increases to 15cm (6in) at the centre, it then narrows using the same frequency back to 10cm (4in) at the top. The whole piece is 20cm (8in) long, so the shaping is worked over 10cm (4in).

When I am shaping, I find a quick sketch of the shape with numbers useful. If you have knitters' graph paper to map this out onto that can really help you work out the shaping because you can count the stitches.

For my shape, I rounded my values to make it a bit easier, starting at thirty needles and increasing to fifty, so that was a difference of twenty needles over forty knitted rows.

This gave a nice easy calculation: I had to increase ten times (20 ÷ 2) over forty rows, giving a frequency of four.

I did the same for the decreases, decreasing by one needle at each edge every fourth row over forty rows.

Use your stitches and rows per cm/inch values to work out how many stitches you need to start with and increase to in the centre, and over how many knitted rows the shaping will occur. When you have these values, you can use the template below to calculate your shaping frequency:

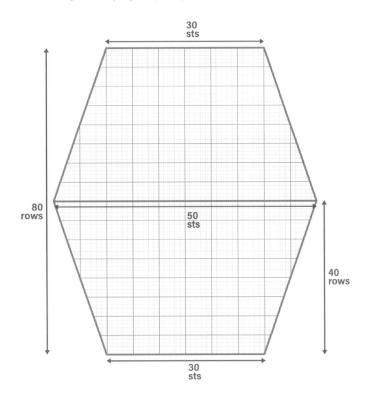

This sketch with numbers gives me a visual of my needles/ stitches and rows and helps make sense of the shaping.

Current stitches, required stitches: Difference = _____

The difference is the number of needles you will be adding for
the increase or reducing by for the decrease

Needles to add or remove = _____

Number of needles to add ÷ 2 = number of times to
increase/decrease

Number of times to increase/decrease = _____

Number of knitted rows to increase/decrease over ÷ number of
times to increase/decrease = shaping frequency

Shaping frequency = _____

Once you have all your values, you can knit the shape. First, make
a note of the following so you have something to follow:

- Starting width in stitches
- Frequency
- Widest point in stitches
- Rows to knit half the shape over

If you like, make a small sketch of the shape. Remember, you will be
increasing or decreasing on both edges of the fabric at each shaping point. You might also want to list the rows that your shaping
occurs on, for example 4, 8, 12, 16 and so on.

That is all the shaping information you need for now, though we
will revisit the topic in Chapter 7. For more shaping and calculation
practice, try knitting the socks at the end of this chapter.

Jacques Agbobly, Black Boy Knits

Jacques in their studio.

My name is Jacques Agbobly and I am a multidisciplinary designer and artist based in New York City. I graduated from the BFA Fashion Design Program at Parsons in 2020, where I focused my studies on materiality, sustainability and indigenous West African handcrafts such as weaving, knitting and beading. I began machine knitting during my second year of school. Shortly after graduating Parsons, I launched my label, Black Boy Knits, where I create unique pieces on a made-to-order basis.

My work explores narratives of the Black immigrant experience by examining the connections between past and present realities that inform Black futures. With these themes in mind, I've strengthened my design focus in colours, materials and silhouettes that subvert gender expectations in order to portray the multiplicity of the Black identity.

What brought you to machine knitting and where did you learn?

I was first introduced to machine knitting during my freshman year of college. The knitting lab was located on the same floor as one of my courses and I could hear the sound of the machines through the walls while studying. One day I walked into the room and saw the machines in action and was immediately obsessed. I then decided to start taking knitting lessons the following semester, where I learned the basics.

Can you tell us about the knitting machines you use now and why they are the right machines for your practice?

I started knitting in 2017 and have owned and operated various machines since then. I currently have three Brother domestic machines – a 970, 965i and 260 bulky machine. During the summer of 2020 I invested in a Passap e6000 machine.

As a small business it is often difficult to outsource to factories due to minimum order quantities so for my practice it is important that I have various machines that are able to create different types of knit structures. I mostly work on my Brother 965i. It is my favourite machine and I find it much easier to operate than the other ones I have.

How about your design process – what inspires you?

The design process for each project is always unique, but I always begin with the materials. I would often have ideas in my head of what kind of materials I want to use/experiment with and then think of the silhouette. I respond to colours and materials the most so it's what I often start with. This process can sometimes involve me going to the library, watching a film or even walking around the city and seeing a colour or material that speaks to me. I then try to mimic or replicate the texture through a process of experimentation with the media that are accessible to me.

When you've got your inspiration, how do you take it from idea to the finished product?

I am always on the go, so usually when I do get an idea, I find it helpful either to write it on my phone or do a rough sketch in my sketchbook, which I carry with me everywhere. When I get to my studio, I would then start doing iterations for the design or testing different techniques on the machine so that I have different options. The best approach to my design process is to do multiple stages of iteration before landing on the final product. After deciding on the knitting technique, I then go through the different phases of pattern making to figure out the specifics of shaping in order to get the correct fit.

A knitted swatch and finished garment in Jacques' studio.

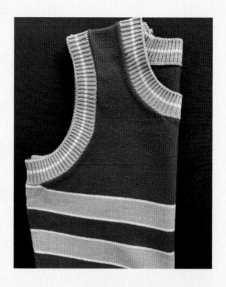

A knitted vest showing fashioning marks created by shaping.

Black Boy Knits collection garments.

Do you have any favourite yarns that you like to work with?
I've knitted using a variety of yarns but my favourite is merino wool. I find this the easiest to knit with on the different types of knitting machines I have. It also makes it easier to switch between machines or use multiple different machines within one garment.

This chapter has been all about shaping. Can you tell us about how you use shaping in your work?
When I first started knitting, I used to avoid shaping like the plague! My brain just couldn't figure out how to calculate the shaping and I dreaded it for so long, especially when it came to partial knitting on the back shoulders to get the slope. After graduating college and getting my own studio space, I was able to put myself in a headspace to tackle this fear and it ultimately became my favourite part of knitting.

Shaping for me is something that makes or breaks the garment. You can have a beautiful design, but if it's not technically finished or shaped well, it can ultimately impact the way your garment looks. I always do fully fashioned shaping, which takes the longest but produces the beautiful marks that we love to see in well knitted garments.

Do you have a favourite transfer tool or method of shaping?
I really love the two-by-three transfer tool. It's what I use for my shaping in order to get the full fashioning marks.

Do you have any hints and tips on shaping?
I am a visual learner, so it's really hard for me to read instructions and follow them. The best way I've been able to learn is through watching a lot of YouTube videos on certain techniques I am struggling with.

Do you have any advice for people who are learning to use a knitting machine? Is there anything you wish you had known when you were starting out?
For beginners, I would say the best thing to do would be to get yourself your own machine. It does not have to be anything fancy or complex – just something you can practise on in your own space at your own pace.

I first started knitting in a course, which was great, but our time on the machines was limited and this impacted my progress. Once I invested in my own machine, it was much easier to keep up and expand my own learning.

Where can people find your work?
🅞 @illinoize and @blackboyknits.
🌐 www.blackboyknits.com

Sour Apple Single Bed Socks

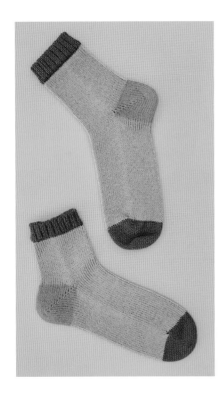

Completed knitted socks using contrast colours on heel, toe and top mock rib trim.

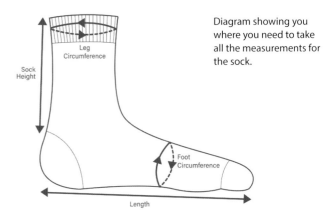

Diagram showing you where you need to take all the measurements for the sock.

method for the yarn – washing and blocking or steaming – and calculate the stitches and rows per cm/inch, making a note of them for this project.

This project applies some of the simple shaping methods you have learnt in this chapter. These socks have been knitted using merino four-ply yarn in green, blue and pink. You can of course knit them in any colours you like.

You will need:
- Yarns to knit the sock
- Waste yarn
- Tape measure
- Transfer tool
- Calculator

TENSION SWATCH

Before you can calculate how many needles and rows you need to knit to make your sock, knit a tension swatch. Remember to include whichever mock rib you would like to use for the cuff of the sock at the beginning of the swatch. Use the appropriate finishing

MEASUREMENTS

The other thing you will need are measurements to make sure you knit the right size of sock for your feet. You will need to measure both your foot and lower leg. Take the four measurements below using a tape measure.

Foot circumference
Measure around your foot at the widest point

Foot length
Measure from the top of your big toe to the back of your heel on the bottom of your foot

Sock height
Measure from the top of the heel area on your sock to where you would like the sock to finish – you can measure this with your favourite socks on

Leg circumference
Measure around your leg where you want the top of the sock to sit.

Converting to Stitches and Rows

Now you need to convert your foot measurements into stitches and rows so you know how many needles to cast on over and how many rows to knit for the foot and leg sections of the sock. When you have got these values, you can then consider any shaping that might be needed between the top of the sock and the foot area.

Foot circumference in cm/inches × sts per cm/inch = number of stitches in foot of sock

_____ cm or inches × _____ sts/cm or inch = _____ sts
This needs to be rounded to an **even** number.

Length in cm/inches × rows per cm/inch = number of rows in foot of sock

_____ cm or inches × _____ rows/cm or inch = _____ rows in foot

Sock height in cm/inches × rows per cm/inch = number of rows in leg of sock

_____ cm or inches × _____ rows/cm or inch = _____ rows

Leg circumference in cm/inches × sts per cm/inch = number of stitches at top of sock

_____ cm or inches × _____ sts/cm or inch = _____ sts
This needs to be rounded to an **even** number.

To give you an idea of the kind of numbers I was working with, my tension was three stitches and 4.4 rows per cm. My foot measures 22cm in circumference and 24cm in length with a leg circumference of 20cm.

So, the values I used for my sock are:

Foot circumference = 22cm × 3 = 66 needles
Length = 24cm × 4.4 = 106 rows
Sock height = 12cm × 4.4 = 52 rows
Leg circumference = 20cm × 3 = 60 needles

Calculating Shaping for the Leg of the Sock

Now you've got the number of stitches (needles) you need to use for the sock to fit your foot and your leg, we need to look at any shaping that you need to do in the leg of the sock.

The socks I knitted are short ankle socks and, as I have wide feet and small ankles, the top of my sock is narrower than the foot. Depending on your foot and leg measurements, these values could be the same, in which case you wouldn't need to shape the leg of the sock. If your proportions are different to mine, or you are knitting longer socks, the leg circumference will likely be larger than the foot circumference, meaning you would decrease over the top of the socks.

The leg of the sock will also include a lifted hem. If you want the top hem to be the same as in the sock pictured and are working with similar four-ply yarn, the lifted hem will be twelve knitted rows high, so you need to take this number away from the number of rows calculated to knit the top of the sock. If you are working with a different hem height, take that number away from the number of rows you have calculated for the sock leg area. Looking at my calculations, that leaves me with forty rows for the top of the sock after knitting the hem.

When you have subtracted your hem rows from your sock leg rows, if you need to shape the leg part of your sock, follow the steps below to calculate your shaping frequency:

1. Find the difference between the leg circumference and the foot circumference in stitches.
2. Divide this by two to find out how many times you will need to increase or decrease using the transfer method,
3. Divide the knitted rows needed for the top of your sock by the number of times you will be increasing or decreasing to find your frequency.

Calculating Foot Length Minus Heel and Toe Areas

The length you have calculated is for the full length of the sock, but we will be knitting a heel and toe into the sock too. Regardless of the size of your sock, your heel and toe combined will take up forty knitted rows of your sock, so for the number of rows you will need to knit, take forty away from the number you had before. For my socks, that makes the length to knit between the toe and heel of my sock sixty-six rows. Make a note of this number.

If you are using a very fine or very heavy yarn, or if you are knitting children's socks, the combined heel and toe might take up more or fewer rows; for this pair, however, try to work to a similar tension to mine.

KNITTING THE SOCKS

Make sure you have a note of all the values from the above calculations:

- Stitches at cuff of sock
- Knitted rows for hem
- Knitted rows for leg of sock (and frequency if needed)
- Stitches at foot of sock
- Knitted rows for length of foot with toe and heel subtracted

Follow these steps to knit your socks:

1. Cast on your required number of stitches using waste yarn, making sure you centre the stitches over the zero on the machine.
2. Knit a mock rib lifted hem in colour 2, remembering the loose row at the start and centre of the lifted hem, and lift this onto the machine needles.
3. Zero your row counter to prepare for knitting the top of the sock.
4. Knit your required number of rows for the leg of your sock, shaping as needed using the frequency from your calculations.
5. Use partial knitting to shape the heel of the sock. First, split the sock in two by pushing half of the needles up into hold position – all the needles on either the left or right side of the zero, depending on which sock you are knitting. You will knit the heel on the left-hand side of your knitting for one of your socks, and on the right-hand side for the other.
6. Follow the partial knitting for sock shaping instructions (*see* section on Partial Knitting on page 92) to knit the heel of your

sock. Don't forget to put the carriage into the hold position over these rows.
7. Set the machine from holding back to knit, and knit the desired number of rows for the length of the sock.
8. Knit the very last row of this section at a stitch size one whole number bigger than the size used for the main part of the sock; this is because these stitches will be rehung onto the machine when we close the toe.
9. Now it's time to shape the toe. Knit this in the same way as the heel up to the row before the last on the same side of the centre as the heel.
10. Knit the last row of this section at a stitch size one whole number bigger than for the rest of the toe; again, this is because these stitches will be rehung onto the machine when we close the toe.
11. Using the waste yarn, switch back from hold to knit, and knit ten rows at the end of the sock across all needles.
12. Knit across with no yarn to remove the whole sock from the machine.
13. Knit the second sock following the same instructions, making sure that you hold the stitches on the opposite side to the previous sock so that the seams will be on different sides of the socks and can be worn on the inside of the legs.

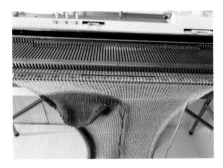

All the sock knitting has been completed and you are ready to join the toe of the sock together.

JOINING THE SOCKS

Now the socks have been knitted, you just need to join each sock up. You can do this on the machine by following the steps below, or by hand if you prefer.

1. First, close up the toe by rehanging only the stitches from the shaped toe onto needles, with the right side of the sock facing you. This is half the number of stitches you have on the waste yarn.
2. Then fold the sock in half so that the purl/back of the fabric is facing you, and place the rest of the stitches held with waste yarn on the same needles. This will result in two stitches on every needle, one from the shaped toe and one from the main body of the sock.
3. Cast these off with the latch tool. The seam will sit inside the sock once turned the right way round.
4. Once the toe seam is complete and the waste yarn taken off, you can join the side seam.
5. To link on the machine, hang all the stitches onto the machine, starting at the stitch at the top of the toe seam and working all the way up to the top of the sock, hanging first one side of the sock then the other on top of it; the inside of the sock will be visible.
6. Join the sock using the latch tool cast-off method. When you reach the lifted hem, simply join the outer half of the lifted hem as with the neck band.
7. When both socks are complete, finish them by washing/ steaming and blocking to shape before wearing them.

VARIATIONS

This sock pattern gives you the instructions to knit a plain block colour sock and is a great starting point. After you have worked through it and successfully made your first pair, you can think about designing your own. Stripes are an easy place to start, but you can also use punch cards in the design, either all over the socks or just in the top area.

Another option is to use hand-transfer lace patterns or a lace punch card if your machine has that capability. Remember, for socks, it is best to work with yarns that have a good amount of stretch and recovery for a good fit; wools and acrylics will usually fit better than cotton.

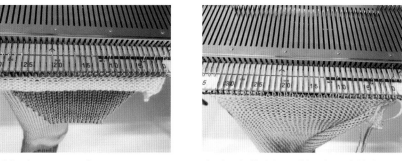

The sock has been removed on waste yarn and the toe half of the sock rehung onto the machine.

The foot half of the sock has been folded over and the stitches hung on top of the toe stitches.

The sock has been joined at the toe, then hung along the edge.

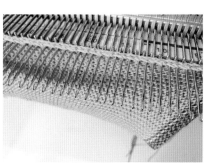

The sock has been folded to bring the other edge up onto the needles.

These socks have been made using a punch card on the leg area and knitted plain on the foot.

CHAPTER 5

COLOUR AND DESIGN

In this chapter we are going to look at using colour again and combining that with more techniques for fabric design. We will start by exploring intarsia and follow this by revisiting partial knitting and exploring how this can be used in fabric design. We will also consider colour application, as well as creating and using a colour palette.

INTARSIA

This technique allows you to create designs with multiple colours in a knitted fabric. Using an intarsia carriage or setting on your carriage and laying yarns in by hand means that there is no limit to the scale and complexity of the design. I often think of intarsia as drawing with yarns; it can take some planning, but the results are limitless.

One of the key features of an intarsia fabric, as opposed to a punch-card fabric, is that there are no floats on the back of the fabric. This technique creates a single-layer knitted fabric with a very neat back. It is much more time-consuming than punch-card patterning but is actually a very easy technique to learn. All you need is a machine with an intarsia setting or a separate intarsia carriage.

These images of a completed garment by KNYT and the back of it being knitted show both the creative potential and working process of intarsia.

How to Knit Intarsia

Rather than just explaining the basics, this how-to section will take you through all the steps needed to create a simple intarsia fabric.

You will need:
- Intarsia carriage/setting
- Three pegs/clips
- Three yarns of different colours

1. Before knitting intarsia, cast on over fifty needles using your favourite technique and whichever colour you want as the central column of colour in your design.
2. When you have cast on, knit eight rows for the bottom solid section of the design. Then either replace your standard carriage with the intarsia carriage, placing it on the left-hand side of your knitting, or set your carriage to knit intarsia.
3. For the intarsia part of this fabric, we will be using three different-coloured yarns, including the yarn you started with; these need to be on the floor in front of the machine, rather than running through the tension arms. This is because none of the yarns go through the yarn feeder. Instead, they are laid into the needles before the carriage is taken across. Cut the yarn you have just been working with and place all three yarns on the floor in the order you will be using them in the pattern; the cast-on colour will be in the middle.
4. To set up the needles for intarsia, pass the intarsia carriage over the knitting area from left to right. The needles will move into upper working position and all the latches will be open. It is important that the carriage is now on the right-hand side of your machine. This is because when you knit intarsia, you need to lay the yarns over the needles in the same direction that you will be moving your carriage.
5. You are now ready to start the intarsia knitting. Starting with the right-hand yarn, place a peg on the end and leave a tail of around 15cm (6in) hanging down over the right-hand side of the edge needle. Lay the yarn that is attached to the cone over the first twenty needles from right to left, placing the yarn on top of the open latches.
6. Now introduce the second yarn. Again, attach a peg and leave a tail, laying this yarn over the next ten needles in the same way as the first yarn.
7. Introduce the third yarn in the same way and lay it over the remaining twenty needles.
8. Now pass the carriage over the knitting area while holding the yarns coming from the cones loosely in your hand to

A simple intarsia fabric using three different colours.

make sure they pass through into the needles smoothly and evenly; the pegs will weigh down the loose ends.
9. Now you will take the yarns back over the needles, starting at the left-hand side, working one yarn at a time from left to right. This time, make sure that they cross each other, bringing the new yarn from underneath the yarn just used. If the yarns don't cross, you will end up with gaps in the knitting; the crossing of the yarns brings the separate-coloured sections together so it is very important.
10. With the yarns laid over and all the yarns coming down on the right hand-side of each knitting area, take your carriage across to knit.
11. With the carriage at the right-hand side, you will now lay the yarns over the needles taking them from right to left. The crossing of the yarns will be more natural in this direction as you are simply untwisting the yarns where they crossed from the previous knitted row. Make sure that the yarn is laid into every needle and the latches are open.
12. In this design, we are sticking to the same number of needles for each colour block the whole way through, so you will simply keep laying over and knitting the yarns in for as long as you want the vertical striped area to be. I knitted sixty rows of intarsia in this sample.
13. When you have knitted your desired number of rows, either change the setting on your carriage or replace the intarsia carriage with the main carriage. Cut all three yarns, leaving enough of a tail to work in and thread the central colour into your main knitting carriage.
14. Now knit the top plain border, working the same number of rows as at the bottom, and cast off.

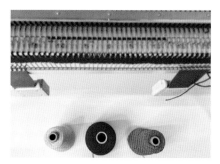

For intarsia knitting, the cones of yarn are placed on the floor in front of the machine so that you can lay them over the needles by hand to create your pattern.

Needles in upper working position ready to lay the yarns over.

Three yarns are laid into the needles for the first knitted row. Make sure all needles have yarn laid in and you haven't missed any.

Here the yarns are laid over the needles to knit the second row, crossing each other where we move from one colour to the next.

The yarns are travelling in the opposite direction as we prepare to take the carriage from right to left.

The intarsia section has been knitted and we are moving back to plain knit using the central colour yarn.

Adding More Colours

Now you can try adding more colours. In the previous example, straight columns were knitted, but you can create anything you can imagine using intarsia, so let's look at creating a design with some diagonal lines that will require you to bring new colours in as you work. This sample will be really good practice if you want to knit the cushion at the end of the chapter, as it has the same diagonal line.

You will need:
- Intarsia carriage/setting
- Six pegs/clips
- Yarns: pink (two ends), yellow (two ends), green, blue

You will use the exact same technique of laying yarns over and making sure you cross them on each pass as you did on the previous sample. This design will use four yarn colours, but you will need multiples of the pink and yellow because they are appearing in more than one place in the same row. You don't need very much

of these colours; I wound a small amount off onto some hand-knit bobbins.

With the first example we didn't need a chart to follow because the design was really simple, but for this design we will use one. Notice how the chart overleaf is a mirror image of the resulting fabric; this is because when you knit intarsia, you are working into the back of the fabric.

Cast on with pink and knit two rows; these will count as the two first rows of the chart. Then follow the chart from row three, bringing the yellow in at one edge. Do the same with the yellow at the end, then knit two rows after working the chart before casting off.

To introduce a new yarn, attach a peg to the loose end and bring the yarn up between the needles in the desired position. To help secure this new yarn, knit the first stitch in by hand, leaving this needle back in working position, then lay the yarn over the remaining needles in the area you want this new colour to appear. When you take the carriage across, the new colour will be knitted in and the needle in working position will just move back to upper working position ready for the next row.

This sample shows how multiple colours can be used in an intarsia design, with different colours being introduced in different areas of the fabric.

Here you can see the yarns laid over the needles on my machine as the diagonal design is being knitted.

Chart showing the diagonal stripe pattern and rows. Simply follow the chart from the bottom up to knit the design.

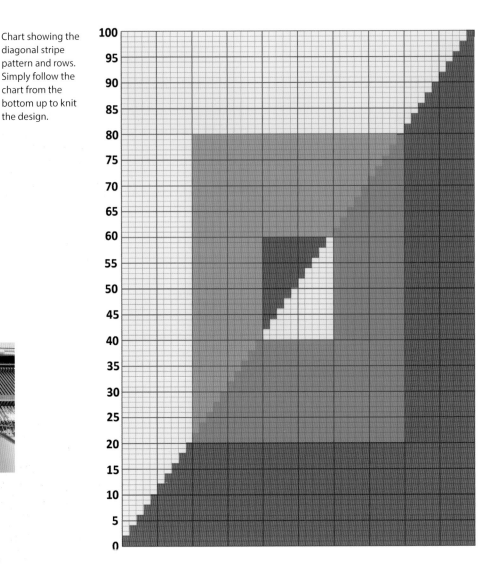

Designing your Own

Once you have had a go at both of these exercises and understand the process, you can have a go at designing your own. Remember, for intarsia designs, you need to work with the design you want on the front of the fabric flipped horizontally on the chart you are following because you work into the back of the fabric.

As with any design, you will need to knit a tension swatch to start with to get an idea of the scale that the design will be, then use knitters' graph paper to sketch out the design. As with all knitting, you are working with a grid, so smooth curves and rounded shapes will be more difficult to achieve than straight lines and angular shapes. Using the knitters' graph paper will help to get an idea of how the shapes are working, and you might start with quite complex shapes that you can simplify as you develop the design. With intarsia work, you will often end up with a rough design on knitters' paper before you get to a neat chart that you will follow.

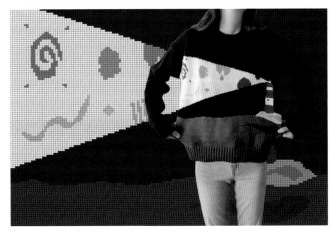

This image from KNYT shows the intarsia graph with the design mapped onto it (flipped so it matches the knit) and the finished jumper in front of it.

PARTIAL KNITTING FOR COLOUR AND SURFACE

We have looked at using partial knitting for shaping, but as this technique allows you to knit some of the needles and not others, it is also great for adding colour to a fabric. There are a few simple techniques that you can use – and easily adapt to create your own designs.

Short-Row Striping

Short-row knitting is a technique we looked at in the previous chapter for shaping the heel and toe areas in the sock; here we are using it to create contrasting areas and irregular stripes to add interest to the fabric.

Short rows add knitting in a selected area of the fabric, so when using it for colour application we need to balance the rows out. This means mirroring what you have done on one side/area of the fabric on the other side/another area of the fabric to keep the fabric as even as possible. I have used the term 'stripe' in this first example because each colour is always carried across the whole fabric.

This first example has been created by knitting a segment at the edge of the fabric, then returning to knit all needles and working across the whole piece of fabric. I have also knitted some plain stripes in between the short-row stripes for extra interest and contrast.

The second sample shows segments knitted in the same way but partial knitting is used with every single colour, and a wider range of colours has been knitted into the sample. This is a very flexible technique with huge potential for design effects; have a play around with colour, segment and stripe combinations to see what you can create.

Colour Pops

As well as working at the edge of the fabric and using partial knitting to create uneven stripes, you can use it to knit small areas of contrast colour anywhere in your fabric. We are going to look at creating small areas of colour in the fabric that will lie flat when pressed.

Because we want these to lie flat, and this can be a tricky technique, we are going to make each shape a maximum of six rows

This sample shows how short rows can be used to create interesting uneven stripes within a fabric.

Multicolour uneven stripes created using partial knitting.

Here we have small areas of partial knitting that are being used to introduce colour into different areas of the fabric.

high. They can be as wide as you like, but if you make them very narrow, there might be a risk they are raised from the surface. My smallest colour pop starts at eight needles wide. To knit these small segments follow these steps:

1. Push up all the needles you don't want to knit into hold position, leaving a section of needles in working position.
2. Change the yarn to the colour you want to use for this section.
3. Hang a weight on the fabric directly below this area.
3. Knit two rows, making sure to pass the yarn under the needle at each edge of the knitting area to prevent holes.
4. When you have knitted two rows, widen the shape by pushing the two edge needles back into upper working position and knit another two rows.
5. To bring the shape back in, narrow the knitting area by bringing the edge needles back into hold position. Do this one edge needle at a time, on the side opposite the carriage, so that they don't knit on the next row. Don't forget to still pass the yarn under the needle next to the knitting area.
6. You will now have knitted six rows and your colour pop is finished. Swap back to the main yarn, set the machine back to the knit setting and knit across.

You can play around with the width of these small pops of colour. Just remember that every time you are knitting one, you are adding rows to the knitted fabric in that area, so try to spread them out regularly over your fabric to maintain an even number of rows over the whole piece. If you want more than one in the same row, simply work another colour pop before knitting the main colour across the row.

Raised Areas

Another great effect you can get using partial knitting is surface texture. As we know, partial knitting is creating extra fabric in a chosen area on your knitting, so if you were to just keep knitting in that area, you would end up with a section that sticks out from the surface. Here we are not passing the yarn under the needles next to the partial knitting areas because we want them to be separate from the base fabric.

There are so many variations you can create when you have got the hang of this technique; here we will just go through creating bobbles and surface loops. When you have mastered these, you can start experimenting to see what you can come up with.

The small raised areas create interesting surface texture – as well as contrast, if knitted in a different colour to the base fabric – and they are quick and easy to knit.

Contrast colour being knitted in a small section of the fabric; so far, two rows have been knitted.

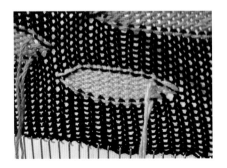

A small, narrow oval colour pop completed using partial knitting.

These two swatches both have raised areas on the surface that have been created with partial knitting – bobbles on the left and surface loops on the right.

These small, raised areas are simple bobbles, sometimes referred to as popcorn stitches.

Knitting Bobbles

1. Push up all needles into hold position except the two where you want to knit the bobble.

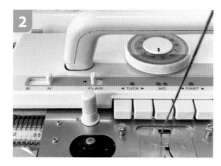

2. Swap your yarn out for the yarn with which you want to knit the bobble, and set the carriage to hold position.

3. Knit six rows using this yarn, remembering to hang a weight directly under this area for tension.

4. Using a two-pronged transfer tool, lift the last two stitches before the start of the bobble onto the two working needles.

5. To knit multiple bobbles in the same row, leave this yarn threaded and push the two working needles on which you just knitted the bobble into hold position.

6. Now place the two needles where you want the next bobble to be into upper working position, then repeat steps 3 and 4 to complete another bobble.

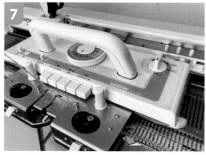

7. When you have knitted the desired number of bobbles on that row, swap back to the original yarn, change the setting from hold to knit, and knit across.

Surface Loops

To create surface loops in the fabric, you start in the same way as when knitting a bobble, but you can knit as many rows as you want and the loops can be wider than two stitches. Also, it is up to you whether you lift the stitches back onto the needle or not; this will create different effects. With both of the surface loop examples shown here, don't pass the yarn under the needles next to the partial knitting area as you don't want these to be attached to the fabric.

That is something you could try out after you have worked through these examples. Simply follow the same steps but pass the yarn under the needles at the edge of the knitting area to attach the raised areas to the main knitted fabric.

Both rows have surface loops that are four stitches wide. On the bottom row, the stitches have not been lifted to close the hole. The top row shows how, by lifting the stitches, the gap is closed and by pressing these down when finishing the fabric, a more flap-like effect is created.

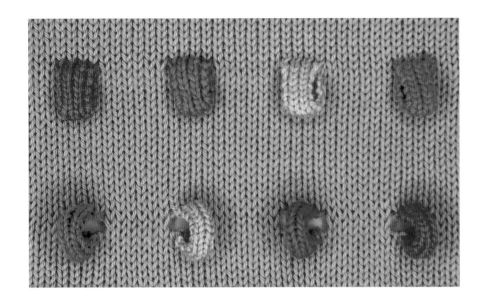

COLOUR AND DESIGN

The goal of this book is to teach you the skills you need to be able to design your own knits, and whether that's simple striped socks or an intarsia jumper, you will need to think about colour. There are a lot of factors that can affect your use of colour in a machine-knitting project. Is it for yourself or someone else? Is it part of a collection that needs to work with other designs? What aesthetic do you want to achieve? Perhaps most importantly, what colours are available in the yarn you want to use?! With all these things in mind, there is often some compromise involved when making colour choices.

When you start the process of designing, you will usually have an idea or flash of inspiration, and whether that comes from the packaging of your favourite childhood sweets or a beautiful landscape, there is usually colour related to that inspiration.

As knitters, we work with a yarn palette, and as discussed right at the beginning of the book, different fibres will give different qualities to the resulting fabric, so deciding on the kind of yarn you would like to use can be a great first step in building a palette for a project.

Each yarn quality will come in a limited number of colours, so I would suggest you decide on the yarn/s you want to use and see what is out there before setting your heart on a specific palette. If you can buy yarns in person that is the best way to do it, as you get a true representation of the colour and yarn quality; if that isn't an option, many machine-knitting yarn suppliers will send you a small sample of a yarn. Once you have the yarns, you can start to knit some palette swatches to help you decide on colours.

These two images show the source of inspiration and a yarn palette that has been created from it.

When you have created a palette swatch, you can decide where the colours will go in your design. You will be knitting tension swatches no matter what the project, and you can always use these to experiment with colour combinations. If the knit involves using a punch card, try the two colours you will be using both ways round to see how the pattern looks. Remember, if you want a subtle effect, choose colours that are close to each other, while stark contrasts create a bolder look. Finally, don't forget you can also mix thinner yarns together to create blended colours.

Lisa McFarland

Lisa in her studio.

Garment in progress on Lisa's knitting machine.

I'm Lisa McFarland and I run LISA-LAND, a small handmade clothing business, out of Oakland, California. I got my first knitting machine in 2014, then dabbled in it for years until I began knitting full time at the beginning of 2020 (pandemic unemployment life-saver!), and started my own business later that year.

What brought you to machine knitting and where/how did you learn?

I was a hand knitter/crocheter and sewer, but never realised domestic knitting machines even existed until I happened upon a photo of one on Instagram. I was instantly amazed and intrigued, and set out researching how and where to get one. I found a local Silver Reed dealer in my area, and purchased a brand-new machine from her directly. She gave me a free intro lesson when I picked up the machine, and I ventured out on my own from there. I watched a lot of videos and studied the manuals and books I could find, then I sought out in-person classes through a local art school's extension program, flew up to Seattle and took a class at the Knitting School, and joined and attended monthly meetings at The Machine Knitters Guild of the San Francisco Bay Area.

However, for most of these years, knitting was on the back-burner and I spent most of my free time sewing. Honestly, I felt very intimidated by my knitting machine. Once I shifted my focus to knitting and practised many or most days of the week, I began to gain the skills and confidence I craved, and started having a lot more fun in the process.

Can you tell us about the knitting machines you use now and why they are the right machines for your practice?

All the machines I own are Silver Reed, and the main machine I use is the SK840 with SRP60 ribber. This is an electronic machine, so I use DAK for patterning and design. I chose this machine because when I was first interested in learning to machine knit, I knew absolutely nothing about it, and didn't want to buy a used machine online that might have broken or missing pieces. I was also excited to buy from a local dealer who could show me the ropes and offer resources. I didn't realise how hard it was going to be, and was picturing that I would be making amazing and intricate intarsia sweaters right out of the gate. I splurged for the electronic machine because I felt it gave me the most options for growth and I'm still happy with my choice.

How about your design process – what inspires you?

I'm inspired by fun fashion from the 1980s and early 90s, which is the time period I grew up in, and have been obsessed with ever since. Commercial and homemade knitwear from this time period blows my mind constantly. It was so bold, playful, full of colour and just wacky – that's what I love to see. I made my first text-based sweater back in 2016 when Bernie Sanders was running for president in the US and I wanted to show support out on the street. Having DAK made it super easy to create my own stitch patterns so I went for it. It was a pretty poorly made basic sleeveless pullover, but I loved it and got a ton of compliments on it. When Bernie ran again in 2020, I pulled the sweater back out and felt re-inspired. That is actually when I started knitting all the time, and moved forward with new text-based knits that evolved from there.

When you've got your inspiration, how do you take it from idea to the finished product?

For silhouette ideas I usually draw in a sketchbook. I will just draw tons of ideas and variations and not necessarily do anything with them, but I find to just let it flow helps unlock your best ideas, not worrying about bad ideas or the constraints of what you think is possible. Then later, when I'm ready to take something to the next level, I'll go back and look through all my doodles and pick something that sticks out.

For colour, I find it so helpful to use digital tools to play around easily and try all kinds of options and combos. I draw a basic shape outline or flat digitally using either Illustrator or Procreate, and use that as a template to make easy mock-ups by filling the shapes with colour or patterns in Photoshop. I use DAK to create my stitch pattern, take a screenshot of one repeat section, take that to Photoshop and create a pattern from it, then do a pattern fill to add it to my garment mock-up. I also play around with trim colours by doing a colour fill on the trim sections. It's super-fast and easy way to test out colours and get an idea of how your finished design will look. If you stick to a custom colour palette with all your actual yarn colours, you can make your idea come to life.

Do you have any favourite yarns that you like to work with?

Right now, I'm mostly working in 100 per cent cotton. It's pretty easy to work with and comes in lots of colours. I have a ton of random second-hand cones of all the fibres that I've collected over the years, so I really need to work though that stuff and make some one-of-a-kind pieces too.

This chapter has been all about using colour and intarsia. Can you tell us about how you use colour in your work, and if you use intarsia knit in any of your designs?

I'm obsessed with bright, bold colours, so unless it's for a custom order, that is all I'm really interested in knitting with. I love finding new or unusual colour combos, and can't get enough of the classics. Currently I'm mainly knitting Fair Isle, which is great but also limiting because you can only use two colours in each row. For most of my Fair Isle, I use at least three colours overall – keeping a solid background colour and swapping out my second colour. I also love making colour block garments, because the knitting can be simplified but the colour expression is so bold. My vision when I acquired a knitting machine was to jump right into making intarsia sweaters, but I got sidetracked with having to learn the basics first and fell into a groove with Fair Isle. I have played around and made swatches, but have yet to fulfil my epic intarsia dream. That's still the plan, though.

An out-of-this-world design featuring text and motifs.

Any hints and tips on choosing colours for a project, or working out which colours to put together?

When I'm trying to find new colour combos, I usually start with taking out a ton of cones and just juggling them around till I find something that excites me. I also like to look on Pinterest or Instagram and make collections for colour inspiration, so if I'm stuck, I'll go back and refer to that. Picking colours based on colour theory is a great jumping-off point if you need a prompt. My favourites are analogous and split complementary.

Do you have any advice for people who are learning to use a knitting machine? Is there anything you wish you had known when you were starting out?

If you're struggling, just keep knitting and knitting and knitting. If you're short of yarn funds, unravel and reknit your practice pieces. Don't try to jump ahead to advanced stuff right away, but once you get the basics down, keep challenging yourself to try new things. And make sure to find a community where you can ask questions and get advice, either locally or online.

Where can people find your work?

🌐 lisa-land.com
📷 @lisaland__

A whole knitted outfit showing that knitwear can be more than just jumpers.

Pick 'n' Mix Intarsia Cushion

Patchwork-effect knitted cushion created using intarsia.

This project allows you to work with a variety of colours as well as giving you the opportunity to knit a whole panel using intarsia. Here, we are moving away from wearable designs and working on a cushion.

You will need:
- Yarns to knit the cushion (I used eight different colours)
- Waste yarn
- Intarsia carriage/machine capability
- Eight pegs/clips to secure yarn ends
- Blocking mat/s and pins
- Tape measure
- Calculator
- Cushion filler 40 × 40cm (15 × 15in)

THE DESIGN

For this cushion, I have worked with a repeating unit, mirrored and repeated in a variety of colours. We will be working with a set front panel size of 104 stitches over 150 rows. You will need to try and adjust your tension to be approximately the same as mine, otherwise the cushion could end up too big or too small.

This will be knitted in one long piece made up of two plain areas that will overlap on the back of the cushion and a patterned intarsia area that will be the front of the cushion. The piece will start with a solid lifted hem that will appear on the back of the cushion and end with a cast-off edge. When the piece has been knitted, you will just need to finish the fabric, work ends in and seam the sides of the cushion to complete it.

Before we get into the knitting, a brief word about the design. For this project, I wanted to offer something flexible that could be used not only in this project but also for other creations. The title 'pick 'n' mix' refers to the flexible nature of the repeating unit used in this design, as well as to the fact that you can use any colours you like in your cushion. The patchwork design allows you to take the single unit that I have created and make your own designs using it. For example, a single rectangle could be used for a knitted pin cushion; two could be knitted vertically for the front of a glasses case and so on. With each repeating unit in the design being quite small, it can also be a great project for using up small amounts of yarn.

TENSION SWATCHES

Unlike in other projects, these tension swatches are being worked to match my tension rather than to calculate stitches and rows from. Also, because the cushion is made up of both standard single-bed knitting and intarsia knitting, you need to knit tension swatches for both of these.

I knitted this cushion using a four-ply merino wool with the stitch size set to 5 on my intarsia carriage and to 4 when working single bed. My tension was 3.2 sts and 4.6 rows per centimetre.

To test your tension for the intarsia section, knit a tension swatch using the 26-stitch chart overleaf and see how it comes out. You can adjust the stitch size to alter your tension as required: if your row and stitches/cm values are too high, increase the stitch size; if your values are too low, tighten the tension (if possible) to increase the number of stitches and rows per cm.

When you have created a tension swatch that you are happy with for the intarsia, you need to knit a tension swatch for the back of the cushion. By changing the stitch size one whole number between my intarsia and main knitting I got the same tension. Have a play around with the stitch size until you get your tensions the same.

This cushion has an envelope closure on the back, so to make sure you have plenty of overlap and the envelope closure sits well when finished. The plain areas are both knitted to two-thirds the length of the front panel, which is 100 rows.

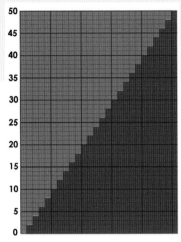

The unit is simply a rectangle that has been divided into two equal triangles using two different colours. This is the chart you will follow to knit your tension swatch.

This is my tension swatch for the intarsia cushion, knitted over twenty-six stitches and fifty rows.

The back of the cushion showing the envelope opening.

KNITTING THE CUSHION

The following instructions to knit the cushion are split into the three sections of the cushion with the intarsia section in the middle. Follow these to knit one large piece of fabric that will be turned into a cushion cover when linked.

Plain Section 1

1. Cast on in waste over 104 needles and knit ten rows.
2. Knit the solid lifted hem as follows: one loose row, fourteen rows, one loose row, fourteen rows, lift hem.
3. Knit length of plain panel: 100 rows ending with a loose row to help with the fold.

Intarsia

1. Place the intarsia carriage on the left-hand side of the knitting area and bring it across from left to right to put all the needles in the correct position.
2. Put all of the yarns you will be using on the floor directly below where you will be working them into the design. I have used eight different colours in each row so that I can work straight from the cones. If you alter the design to repeat a colour in any one row, you will need to wind off some of the yarn onto an empty cone or bobbin to work with.
3. Attach a peg or clip to the loose end of the yarn, and, working from right to left, follow the chart to lay all the yarns over the corresponding needles for the first row of the pattern.
4. Pass the carriage across slowly for this first row, making sure that all the yarns are feeding up from the floor smoothly.
5. For the second row, lay the yarns over the exact same needles, working from left to right, making sure you cross the yarns over each other as you go to avoid holes.
6. When you have done this, pass the carriage over to knit the second row.
7. Continue in this way, following the chart to lay the yarns over the correct needles as you go, taking care to make sure you don't miss any needles. Keep doing this until you have knitted fifty rows; this takes you to the end of the first pattern block.
8. Cut the yarns and use pegs to weigh these loose ends down.
9. Lay over the yarns in the same way you did at the start of the first block, using the attached pegs to secure the ends, and follow the chart to knit the fifty rows of this pattern block.
10. Finish the second block in the same way you did the first. Move on to the third pattern block and knit this in the same way as the first two.
11. When you reach the end of this last block, again cut the yarns and use pegs to weigh them down.

Plain Section 2

1. Switch carriages or change the carriage setting back to standard knitting, and thread the relevant yarn for this section.
2. Starting with a slightly looser row, knit 100 rows for this section.
3. Cast off using your favourite method.

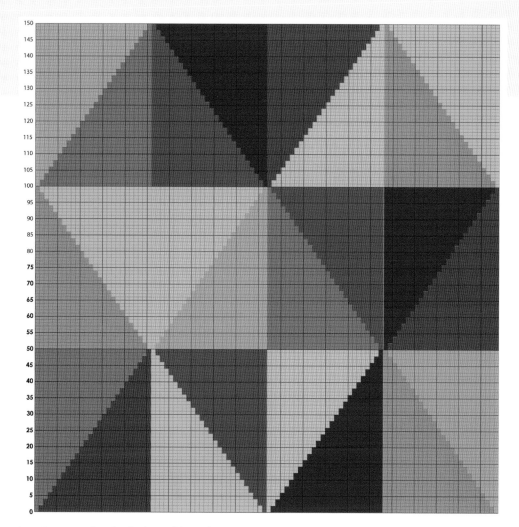

150
145
140
135
130
125
120
115
110
105
100
95
90
85
80
75
70
65
60
55
50
45
40
35
30
25
20
15
10
5
0

Intarsia pattern chart for the front of the cushion.

Yarns laid over the needles for the first intarsia row.

First pattern block knitted.

Yarns laid over the needles for the first row of the second block.

Intarsia panel completed on the machine.

Cushion hung onto the machine ready to be joined.

FINISHING AND CONSTRUCTION

Finishing

1. Sew in all loose ends on the back of the intarsia.
2. Finish the fabric as required, washing if needed, and block in sections.
3. Gently press the fabric along the folds into position.

Construction

1. Hang the intarsia section onto the machine with the front of the fabric facing you; I hung it over ninety needles.
2. Fold the section with the lifted hem and hang that over two-thirds of the needles.
3. Fold the remaining section and hang over two-thirds of the needles.
4. Push all needles up into hold position and knit across.
5. Link this edge using the latch tool cast-off method.
6. Follow the same steps to join the other edge of the cushion. Place a cushion filler inside and it is ready to use!

CHAPTER 6

LEVEL UP – RIBBER

USING THE RIBBER

In this chapter we are moving from working on a single bed to using the ribber and working on a double bed. There is a lot you can achieve without a ribber bed, but to get a true rib fabric that has good stretch and recovery properties, you will need one. Some domestic knitting machines, such as the Passap, have a fixed double bed, but this book focuses on machines that work with a separate ribber bed alongside your main knitting machine needle bed.

The ribber bed comes with its own carriage, as well as different-shaped clamps to raise the main needle bed, a ribber plate that replaces the single bed sinker plate and attaches to the ribber-bed carriage, and two setting plates. Use your manual or a video to guide you in attaching the ribber to your knitting machine; this can feel a bit tricky, but once it's on you can leave it there and just drop it down when you aren't using it. The levers at the sides of the ribber bed allow you to lift the bed easily when you want to use it.

Other accessories that you will need to work with the ribber bed are a double-bed cast-on comb and some hanging weights to use with it. These are quite different to the single-bed combs; they have a wire that passes through a series of holes in the comb and some large holes in the bottom to hang weights from. They come in different sizes, and you will probably want one smaller and one longer one so that you have options.

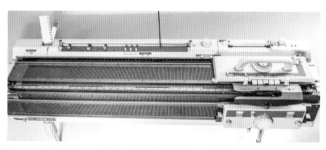

Domestic knitting machine with ribber bed attached.

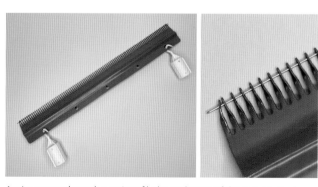

A wire passes through a series of holes at the top of the cast-on comb. Weights with hooks on the top hang on the holes at the bottom of the comb.

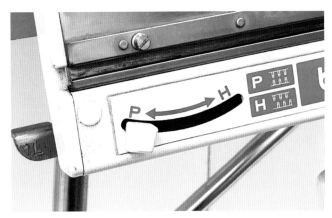

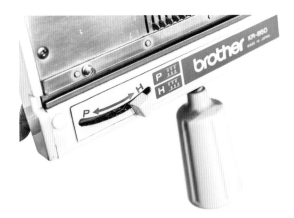

This switch allows you to move the ribber bed so that the needles can sit either in half pitch or directly opposite each other.

The racking handle allows you to move the ribber bed.

On the ribber bed, you will see that there are different positions that the needle bed alignment can be set to. For knitting on all needles, you will want the bed set so that each needle is opposite a gate peg rather than another needle, as this could cause problems when knitting with the needles clashing.

Check your machine's manual to find the relevant switch/setting for your machine. For casting on, you will sometimes use the other position that aligns the needles directly opposite each other. It is worth finding the needle-bed setting switch and having a go at moving the ribber bed position to see how the needles line up when it is moved.

The final thing to note about the ribber bed is the racking handle, which is inserted into the ribber bed. Turning the handle allows you to move the ribber bed in relation to the main needle bed. This is used when casting on for a two-by-one or two-by-two needle rib, and to create decorative effects when knitting rib fabrics. Give it a turn to see what happens before you start using the ribber bed.

CASTING ON

Before we can knit anything using the ribber bed, we need to look at casting on. This is quite different to casting on to a single bed, but it is straightforward and can be quick once you have got the hang of it. There are a few different ways that you can cast on using a ribber bed; I am going to go through the two ways that I use the most and find most successful.

Tubular Cast-on

1. For this tubular cast-on example, we are working a one-by-one needle rib, so you need to start with the ribber bed set with the needles opposite each other.

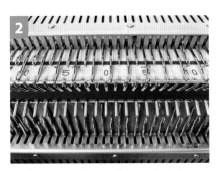

2. Select every other needle over the knitting area you are working on. Ribber needles should all having a corresponding main-bed needle one position over.

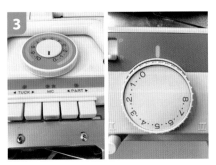

3. Set the stitch size as low as possible, turning the dial past zero on both the main and ribber beds, and set both the main and ribber carriages to knit (check your manual for exact settings).

4. With the yarn threaded, take the carriage across to work the first row. This will lay yarn into all the needles in working position, in what is often referred to as the zig-zag row (you can see why).

5. Now insert the comb. First remove the wire, then bring the comb up from underneath the machine with the teeth between the yarn. Make sure the knitting is in the centre of the comb.

6. Insert the wire back into the comb to secure it to the fabric; this can be fiddly but gets easier with practice. When you have the wire in, hang the weights onto the comb.

7. Next you will knit tubular. To set up, press in one part button on the main carriage and the opposite part button on the ribber bed. Here we have the L button on main and R button on ribber carriage.

8. Leaving the stitch size setting as it is, knit three rows of tubular knit. This setting knits around the comb, allowing it to drop down a bit so it doesn't get stuck in the needles when knitting the rib.

9. Turn off the part settings on both beds so that all needles will knit, increase the stitch size to the desired number and knit the rib. The stitch size is usually half the value of a single-bed fabric in the same yarn.

When you have knitted the rib and taken your knitting off the machine, remove the comb by taking the wire out; you will notice that the very bottom edge of the rib is slightly wavy or flared. This will relax when steamed or washed, but our second cast-on method can help to avoid this.

Draw-Thread Cast-on

This method, known as the draw-thread cast-on, involves casting on with a different yarn and knitting a draw thread, but you need to know how to do the regular cast-on in order to do it, which is why I covered that first. In this example, I have used the waste yarn to knit the draw thread as it involves fewer steps.

You will notice a difference between the tubular and draw thread cast-on edges, with the latter being tighter. Another tip for making your rib nice and tight is to increase the stitch size gradually from zero up to the desired stitch size when moving from tubular to rib knit. To do this, go up one click per row until you get to the desired size. This doesn't work for all yarns, but is good for any thinner and/or more flexible yarns; for example, it will work with a four-ply acrylic but not with a cotton of the same thickness – the cotton needs a larger stitch size straight away, as it is not as elastic.

1. To cast on with the draw-thread method, start by casting on using a waste yarn and the tubular method; I usually use a thinner yarn for this as it will be easier to remove. Now knit a few rows of rib using this yarn.

2. Turn off the main carriage by altering the settings on this carriage, and knit two rows just on the ribber bed.

3. Now set the main carriage to knit again, and knit one row on all needles – this row will be your draw thread.

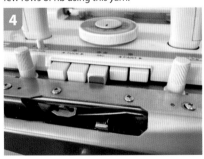

4. Take the yarn out of the feeder, turn off the main carriage and move it over your knitting; this will knock off all the stitches on the ribber bed.

5. You now have loose stitches on the main bed and no stitches on the ribber bed. Change to your main yarn.

6. Set both carriages to knit and your stitch size to below zero, then knit across using the main yarn to begin your cast-on.

7. Change to tubular setting and knit two rows tubular at this tightest stitch size before knitting the rib as usual.

8. Remove the fabric from the machine and cut the large loop at the end opposite the draw-thread yarn tail.

9. Pull the draw thread out to remove the waste from the main knitted fabric.

CASTING OFF

You usually choose to knit ribs because you want the fabric to have stretch in it. With that in mind, you need to make sure that the cast-off isn't too tight, so the fabric still has some elasticity; you can use any cast-off method to do this, but the important thing is to knit a loose row before you start casting off. To get a neat cast-off edge, I like to use the loop-through-loop method, so we are going to go through this here too.

Cast-off edge on a rib-knitted fabric.

Loop-Through-Loop Cast-off

Before you cast off, to make sure the loops don't become too tight, knit one loose row at the end of your piece. Then increase the stitch size by three whole numbers on both the main and ribber bed carriages and knit one row. You want the carriage to finish at the opposite side to the side from which you like to start your cast-off; I cast off right to left, so for this method I end with the carriage on the left.

Loose knitted row before casting off.

Now you have knitted this row, transfer all the ribber bed stitches onto the empty needles on the main bed. This is straightforward when you are knitting a one-by-one rib. With other ribs, where you don't have the same number of ribber-bed stitches as empty needles on the main bed, you just transfer onto both empty needles and needles with stitches on. The important thing is to fill the empty needles.

Ribber-bed stitches transferred to the main bed in preparation for cast-off.

When you have transferred all the stitches to the main bed, you will cast off. Before you do this, drop the ribber bed down so you can get to the main bed easily, and remove the weights from your comb.

The photo sequence goes through how to work the loop-through-loop method. Essentially, this is exactly what it sounds like – you are simply pulling each stitch from the machine through the previous one to close the top of the fabric.

1. To start the loop-through-loop cast-off, push the needles with stitches up towards you so that all stitches are sitting behind the latches.

2. Using the latch tool, pick up the first stitch in the hook of the tool and push the empty needle away from you into a non-working position.

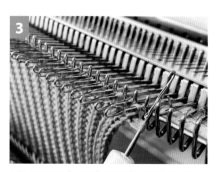

3. Now move the tool upwards so that the stitch moves down the tool and opens the latch.

continued on the following page

4. Place the hook of the tool into the stitch on the next needle along.

5. Now pull this stitch towards you, lifting it and bringing it off the needle. It can help to push the needle that the stitch is on away from you at the same time.

6. Keep pulling the new stitch towards you until the existing stitch closes the latch and the new stitch travels through it; loop through loop. Repeat steps 3 to 6 until you get to the end of your knitting area, and tie off as usual.

RIB LAYOUTS

So far, we have been looking at casting on one-by-one ribs, but there are lots of other ribs you can knit. Another common choice is an all-needle rib; this is exactly what it sounds like – a rib fabric that is knitted on all the needles in your chosen knitting area. This gives a dense and thick rib fabric, but won't have as much stretch and recovery as a one-by-one rib layout.

The one-by-one replicates the knit-one purl-one rib often used in hand knit, and gives a more elastic quality to the resulting fabric. Another popular rib layout is a two-by-one, where you have two needles in working position and one out of working position. I would recommend that you have a go at all three of these layouts, making a swatch of each to see the different fabric quality you get.

To cast on for a two-by-one rib layout, the needles to be arranged as follows: two in working position, one in non-working position across the desired number of needles on both the main and ribber beds. This cast-on also requires the needle bed to be racked by one position in order for the stitches to all knit correctly. To do this you simply start with a two-by-one needle set-up but with the needles crossing each other, and your needle bed set at H, or half pitch.

Knit across once to lay the yarn into the needles, then knit the tubular rows for your cast-on. Before closing the tubular cast-on, rack the needle bed one position to the left so that you have a true two-by-one needle layout with an empty needle opposite each pair of needles with knitted stitches on them.

You can now proceed to knit the rib, making sure you move any single stitches at the edge over to the back bed first to maintain the rib layout, and adjust the stitch size to the required setting for your yarn. When the knitting is off the machine, you will see the difference in appearance between this two-by-one and a one-by-one knitted rib.

From top to bottom, these are an all-needle, a one-by-one and a two-by-one rib fabric, all knitted in the same yarn at the same tension.

This is the position that the needles need to be in to cast on for a two-by-one rib so that the needles can all create knitted stitches.

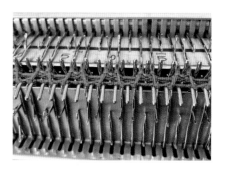

Needle bed racked to move the stitches so that they are in the correct position to create a two-by-one rib.

FROM RIB TO SINGLE BED

There are some knits where you will be using the ribber bed for the whole piece, but more often you will probably have a ribbed trim that then goes into a single-bed knitted fabric. To move from knitting a rib fabric to a single-bed fabric, you simply transfer all the stitches on the ribber bed onto the main needle bed. If you have a rib placement that isn't all-needle knit, you will have some empty needles on the main bed; make sure you transfer stitches onto these empty needles so that every needle has a stitch on it.

When all the stitches have been transferred, remove the ribber carriage and sinker plate and drop the ribber bed. Put your main needle-bed sinker plate back onto the main bed carriage and you are ready to knit your single-bed fabric.

RIB EFFECTS

So far the different rib layouts we have looked at have all been 'true' ribs; they have inherent stretch and are either worked over all needles or have needles out of action to create different rib layouts. We will now look at how you can use the ribber bed to create a surface rib that gives a decorative effect; using a transfer tool to move the stitches gives you a lot of scope for creating your own designs using these methods.

Relief Pattern Using Rib

This is a very versatile effect that uses transferred stitches on the front bed to create areas of both knit and purl stitches on the front face of the fabric, with every needle working on the main bed. In the raised areas, the stitches on the ribber bed are left in working position, keeping the thicker rib quality of the fabric here with

single-bed fabric in between. A simple surface-rib fabric using one colour will simply add texture to the fabric, but this technique can also be combined with plating, racking (*see* below) and further stitch transfer to create a wide variety of fabrics.

Surface rib close-up showing the raised areas created using the rib technique.

All-needle rib transferred into surface rib to create surface texture.

Stitches transferred to the main bed in the desired layout for surface rib design.

To create this effect, you simply choose the kind of relief pattern you want to create, and move the stitches that don't need to be used on the ribber bed from there onto the main bed, and put the empty needles into non-working position. Before knitting the surface rib fabric, put the main-bed stitch size up by a click or two; because there are some areas that are knitting just on the main bed with no ribber stitches, they need a bit more yarn.

This effect may be called a surface rib, but this doesn't mean that the transfers and effect need to be in even sets, or in a repeat across the fabric. A surface rib can be made up of any number of needles knitting on both beds, and any number transferred to knit single-bed fabric, so irregular patterns can be created easily. Remember to increase the stitch size on the main bed, especially if there are large areas where needles have been transferred from the ribber bed to create single-bed fabric.

TOP TIP

To keep the edges from curling, leave the edge stitches on both beds knitting a rib.

Plating

This effect involves using two yarns at the same time to create two-colour effects in rib fabrics. Before you can knit a plated fabric, you need to replace the standard feeder on the ribber sinker plate with a plating feeder. Simply unscrew the standard feeder and put the plating feeder in its place, securing it with the screws.

When you are choosing the yarns for this technique, you need to think about their thickness and flexibility as you are using two at once. If you use two-ply yarns, for example, you would need to work at a bigger stitch size and would get a much thicker fabric than when using a single end of two-ply yarn. There is a limit to how thick the yarn can be for plating to work, because if the combination of the two yarns you choose is thicker than the machine needles can take, it will not knit. For these swatches I used fine one-ply yarns and knitted them at a very low stitch size, just above zero.

You also want the yarns to be as close to each other in thickness as possible for each colour to be visible in the resulting fabric. You can use plating in a full rib fabric, but it won't be visible on the face of the fabric – it will only be evident when you stretch the fabric out.

Surface rib with plating.

While plating does work with a true rib, you can't see the effect very well, and it is most effective when used with a surface rib layout, with one colour being more prominent on the rib area and the other more visible in the single-bed-knitted sections. There is also a lot of scope for altering the design by swapping the position of the yarns around in the two holes of the plating feeder as well as changing colours to use different yarns in the same knitted swatch.

The plating feeder has two distinct sections in which to place two different yarns.

Plating feeder used to knit a one-by-one rib trim; the second colour is hidden in the rib.

These surface rib fabrics have been created using the plating feeder and racking. The yarn positions have been swapped over to change where the colours appear in the fabrics.

Racking

If you have tried a two-by-one or two-by-two rib layout, you will have used the racking handle; if not, then have a go with it to see what happens to the ribber bed when you turn it. The main bed stays in the same position while the ribber bed moves either to the left or right, depending on which way you turn the handle.

When knitting a rib fabric, this motion shifts the ribber bed stitches in relation to the main bed stitches and can bring some movement into your rib knitted fabric. You can rack an all-needle rib fabric, but the movement isn't as visible as when you rack a mock rib, which has better definition.

When racking a knitted fabric there are a few things to keep in mind:

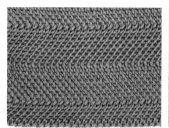

The fabric on the left is an all-needle fabric with racking, and that on the right is the same yarn and same racking pattern but with stitches transferred to create a surface rib.

- Although you can move the bed multiple positions when it is empty, when you are knitting you will move it just one position at a time before knitting at least one row and racking again.
- Only ever rack when the carriage has cleared the knitting area and all the needles are back down in working position so they don't catch each other when racking.
- The number of rows you knit between each rack will affect the pattern that is created on the surface of the fabric.
- Because the stitches are moving each time you rack, you will also need to keep a close eye on the stitches at the edges of the fabric to make sure they aren't dropping.

As with any surface rib, the effect can also be enhanced by combining it with plating to make the surface ribs more obvious.

These two samples show how the number of rows between racking can affect the movement of the mock rib: the pink sample had one knitted row in between each rack and the green sample two.

Moving Ribs

As well as setting up in a surface rib layout and knitting straight surface ribs, it is also possible to move these stitches around. This is done by simply moving the stitches on the ribber bed to different needles; surface rib areas can also be narrowed or widened to create different shapes by adding or removing needles on the ribber bed. To practise moving ribs, a diamond shape is a good place to start working on moving specific stitches in opposite directions. Follow the steps below:

1. Cast on forty needles in full needle rib.
2. Leave the first four stitches at the edge on the ribber bed, transfer fourteen stitches to the main bed, leave the central four stitches on the ribber bed, transfer the next fourteen to the main bed and leave the last four stitches on the ribber bed. Knit a few rows.
3. Using the two-pronged transfer tool, move two stitches one position to the right and two stitches one position to the left.
4. Knit two rows.
5. Repeat steps 3 and 4 over a total of fourteen rows until there are fourteen empty needles in between these stitches. This is the mid-point of the diamond.
6. Knit two rows.
7. Move the same stitches using the two-pronged tool, now bringing them back towards each other.
8. Knit two rows.
10. Repeat steps 7 and 8 over a total of fourteen rows until the stitches meet in the centre of the fabric.

When you have had a go at this and understand the principles of moving ribs, you can start to experiment and see what kind of shapes you can create. As well as transferring the stitches you have left in the surface rib, you can also add or remove stitches from the ribber-bed knitting area/s.

To reduce the surface-rib knitting area, simply transfer the stitch either onto the adjacent ribber-bed needle or onto the main needle bed. To increase it, introduce a needle next to the surface rib by pushing it up into working position and pulling the previous loop from the adjacent needle onto it. Once you start adding and removing stitches from the knitting area, you can become very creative with the surface rib designs you create.

A surface rib has been knitted with the central bank of four needles split and moved to create a diamond shape.

Stitches have been transferred, right-hand stitches to the right and left-hand stitches to the left, putting empty needles down into non-working position after every transfer.

Marta Nowak – Novvaks Knits

Marta wearing one of her creations.

A graphic jumper design with a contrast hem created using the ribber.

I got my BFA in textile design at the Rhode Island School of Design, which is where I was taught textile disciplines such as weaving, dyeing and knitting. My passion for knitting led me to partaking in an artist residency in Brooklyn at the Textile Arts Center, where I was able to fine-tune my knitting expertise and realise a passion for sweater design. I started my Instagram account for Novvaks Knits that same year while living in Brooklyn, and eventually started to sell some of my creations.

What brought you to machine knitting and where/how did you learn?
I learned how to machine knit at school (RISD) on a Brother domestic machine. I originally learned how to hand knit when I was a child, so it was fun to apply the hand-knitting techniques I already knew into what I was learning about in machine knitting. To be frank, it was difficult for me to learn machine knitting. One has to be able to understand the nuances of not only knitting itself, but of the machine (and how it is designed to function). When I first started learning, there were countless times I was unable to correct a mistake or avoid a problem, simply because I still had an untrained eye. I learned that the key to working with this machine is simply patience. Once I mastered the rules of the machine – that's when I was able to experiment with my knitting and find playful ways to break those rules.

Can you tell us about the knitting machines you use now and why they are the right machines for your practice?
I use a domestic Brother knitting machine KH864 and ribber KR850. This is the machine I was taught to use, and find that it is the most accessible to learn on because it is portable and most commonly used for beginner knitting courses.

How about your design process – what inspires you?
Truthfully, colour inspires me. I originally used to paint habitually in my spare time, and was an aspiring painter for most of my teenage years. This passion has transferred into knitting, as I was amazed at the way that touch can influence colour. I find that I am a very tactile person. I loved to hand knit (sew, crochet, embroider, hand weave – all textile-related activities!) occasionally when I was a kid, but I finally realised that machine knitting was my outlet for combining colour and texture in a way that spoke to me. It was during my time at RISD that at last, I realised I can knit wearable and touchable paintings that have no bounds.

As for artists, I am greatly inspired by the work of Anni Albers, for her magnificent sense of colour. I would also include in my top three favourite artists Annie Larson, whose technique and sense of composition is unworldly, and Olivia Herrick, whose work in print design celebrates colour and mindfulness in a way that encourages me to never give up.

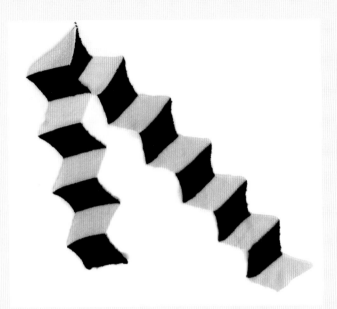

This playful zig-zag scarf has been knitted using the ribber.

Another bold jumper with interest added in the two-colour rib trims.

When you've got your inspiration, how do you take it from idea to the finished product?

I usually start in my sketchbook on gridded paper. I draw along the lines of the grid in angles, because it is much simpler to convert the drawing into a knitting pattern this way, and draw motifs or shapes that I find playful. Sometimes I will draw a whole composition on paper, then play with markers to experiment with colour. Moving onwards, I create a vector file on Illustrator of my pattern to specify it to the correct proportions. I always knit a sample first to see how the colours look – I swear the yarns look different on a cone versus the knit. If I like my sample, I go for it and knit a sweater with that design.

Do you have any favourite yarns that you like to work with?

I love any protein fibre, because I find that when they are dyed, they tend to have the most vibrant colours. I usually work with mohair, because the fuzziness of the fibre can create a fun halo effect on the yarn. Occasionally I will mix with some wools too!

This chapter has been all about using the ribber bed. Can you tell us about how you use the ribber bed in your work, and if you have any favourite methods/effects that you create using it?

I mainly use the ribber bed to make hems (in fisherman rib, also known as brioche rib) for my sweaters and also to make jacquard knits for hats – I love knitting hats with a ribber. I usually knit hats with fisherman rib, full rib and jacquard. Sometimes I will incorporate ottomans too!

Any hints and tips for people working with the ribber bed?

If the carriage gets jammed, clean it – even if it looks clean, clean it. If you don't have sufficient weight, it's always handy to push the needles you are working with all the way up, as this will ensure the stitch jumps off the hook properly to knit. Also, don't be afraid to replace needles, as it's easier than it seems. Most of all, be patient, or try to take breaks!

Do you have any advice for people who are learning to use a knitting machine? Is there anything you wish you had known when you were starting out?

When I first learned how to knit on a machine, I absolutely hated it and did not have the patience. I was so frustrated with why my machine wouldn't work, when I just didn't know its language yet. It takes time to learn, but once you do, it is hard to forget and it is so rewarding for the soul.

Something I wish I knew is that there are always new techniques to learn in knitting, and always new milestones to reach in your craft. Appreciate your old work and how it built you up to become who you are! If you spend a lot of time on a project and it isn't perfect, that's okay. It's part of the learning process, and makes your work unique.

Where can people find your work?

🌐 novvaksknits.com/
📷 @novvaks_knits
♪ @novvaks_knits

Bubble Yum Headband and Hand-Warmers

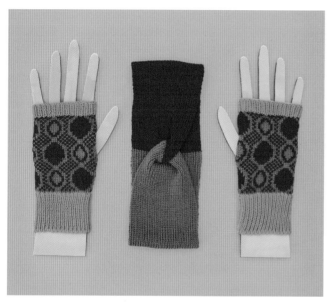

Knitted headband and hand-warmers.

MEASUREMENTS

To make these to the size that is right for you, you will first need to take some measurements.

Hand Measurements

We will start with the hand-warmers. For these, you first measure around your palm just above your thumb joint to get the circumference; this will be the width of the section knitted using the punch card.

For the length, I have made the hand-warmers 19cm (7.5in) long. To work out how long you need yours to be, measure from where you would like the hand-warmer to start on your arm to where you would like it to finish on your hand.

Head Measurement

The other measurement you will need is for the headband. Measure around your head where you want the band to sit, making sure the tape is snug to your head. If the band is a bit small it will stretch, but if it's too big it might slip off.

I have knitted the band 10cm (4in) wide, but it's up to you how wide you make yours. If you already have a headband that you like the width of, measure that.

TENSION SWATCHES

For these projects, you will knit a tension swatch for the hand-warmers and one for the headband. You need one for each as you will be using a punch card for the hand-warmers, so that needs to be included, and we will be using a different yarn for the rib headband.

Practise using your ribber by knitting these two very simple projects. The hand-warmers are knitted with a rib bottom and top, so that they fit snugly to your hands and keep the heat in, and have a punch-card patterned area to make them look fancy. The whole headband is knitted in rib, making it stretchy and thick to keep your ears warm. I have knitted these using the same yarns as the scarf in Chapter 2 so that they all match.

You will need:
- Yarns to knit the headband and hand-warmers (three colours)
- Punch card for the hand-warmers
- Pins
- Transfer tool
- Large sewing needle
- Blocking mat and pins
- Tape measure
- Calculator

Hand-warmers tension swatch.

Headband tension swatch.

Hand-Warmers Tension Swatch

This tension swatch not only gives you the values you need to calculate how many needles and rows you will knit your hand-warmers over, it also allows you to practise working with the ribber and moving from ribber to single bed and back again, as well as casting off.

1. Cast on in a one-by-one rib layout using the draw-thread method and waste yarn. Change to the yarn you will be using for the rib and knit twenty-four rows. I knitted this rib on stitch size 2.
2. Transfer all the stitches to the main bed, drop the ribber bed and replace the ribber plate with the main-carriage sinker plate. Feed your chosen punch card into the feeder and set up to knit Fair Isle. Knit forty rows in your two-colour punch-card pattern. I knitted this on stitch size 4.
3. Change back to your rib colour and knit one row at one whole number above the stitch size you used for the punch card on the main carriage.
4. Remove the main-carriage sinker plate and bring the ribber bed back up into position, then transfer every other stitch onto the relevant needle on the ribber bed to create a one-by-one rib layout. Attach the ribber plate and thread the yarn into here.
5. Knit ten rows of rib, transfer all stitches to the main carriage and cast off using the loop-through-loop method.
6. Finish this swatch in the appropriate way for your yarn by washing and blocking or just steaming, then calculate the stitches and rows per centimetre/inch in the punch-card

area. If you are happy with the size of the ribbed parts, you can just knit the same number of rows when you come to make the hand-warmers; if not, measure to get the rows per cm/inch and use this information to adjust the number of rows you will knit in the ribbed areas.

Headband Tension Swatch

This headband will be worked in a one-by-one rib, but using the colours that you used in the punch card rather than the colours used in the rib for the hand-warmers.

1. Cast on over fifty needles, twenty-five on the main and twenty-five on the ribber bed in one-by-one rib layout.
2. Knit six rows in colour 1.
3. Knit two rows in a contrasting colour.
4. Knit fifty rows with colour 1.
5. Knit fifty rows with colour 2.

Rib fabric showing thirteen stitches over 5cm (2in) on the left, and the same fabric being knitted on the right. Remember, if you count thirteen stitches on one side of the fabric in a one-by-one rib, you need thirteen on the ribber and thirteen on the main bed, doubling the total number of stitches in the fabric.

6. Knit two rows in a contrasting colour.
7. Knit six rows in colour 2.
8. Cast off using the loop-through-loop method.
9. Finish the fabric in the required way for the yarns you are using by washing and blocking or just steaming, and measure the swatch to find out the stitches and rows per cm/inch for this fabric. When you are looking at the stitches, remember whatever the number of stitches you are seeing on the surface of the fabric, there are twice that number of needles knitting due to the rib layout we have used.

CALCULATIONS

For this project the calculations are very straightforward, as there is no shaping involved in either of these pieces.

Hand-Warmer Calculations

First, you will work out over how many stitches you need to knit the hand-warmers. To do this, take the stitches per cm/inch value that you calculated from the tension swatch and multiply it by the circumference of your hand.

Total stitches = stitches per cm/inch × circumference of hand in cm/inches

You will also need to work out over how many rows to knit your hand-warmer. This is split up into three sections as listed below; the lengths of my sections are 6cm for the rib cuff, 11cm for the punch card and 2cm for the rib top.

Rib cuff rows = length of section in cm/inches × rows per cm/inch
Punch-card rows = length of section in cm/inches × rows per cm/inch
Rib top rows = length of section in cm/inches × rows per cm/inch

Headband Calculations

You will use your head circumference measurement to get the number of knitted rows in the headband. As it is being knitted using two large blocks of colour, one for each half of the headband, you need to divide this number by two to get the number of rows you need to knit in each colour.

Total stitches = stitches per cm/inch × width of headband
Total rows = rows per cm/inch × circumference of head
Rows per colour = total rows ÷ 2

Make a note of all the values.

MAKING THE HAND-WARMERS

Knitting Step-by-Step

1. Cast on in waste using the draw-thread method over the required number of needles in one-by-one rib layout.
2. Knit the required number of rows in rib for the cuff.
3. Transfer the stitches to the main bed, change to knitting on the main carriage only by swapping the sinker plate and dropping the ribber bed, then knit the punch card as you did for the tension swatch; knit the required number of rows.
4. Return to normal knitting, change to rib yarn and knit one row at a looser tension.

Hand-warmer pinned before linking.

Completed hand-warmers.

5. Bring the ribber bed up, transfer into one-by-one rib and swap to the ribber sinker plate.
6. Knit a length of top rib, knitting the last row at three numbers larger than the rib stitch size.
7. Cast off using the loop-through-loop method.
8. Finish the fabric before construction.

Construction

1. Measure over the thumb area of your hand to find out how big a gap you want to leave for your thumb.
2. Pin the hand-warmer together inside out, leaving a gap for your thumb, and try it on. Adjust the pinning if needed.
3. Place pins to mark the gap as you did with the shoulder seams for the jumper (*see* Chapter 3's project).
4. Join the seams using your preferred method (on machine or hand-linking). Seam up to the pin, tie off and cut the yarn, leave the gap for your thumb, then join the remainder of the hand-warmer above this point.
5. You can either join the seams on the machine using the same process you have for all previous construction, or by hand; as the seamed areas are quite small, the latter can be quicker.
6. When the seams have been joined, turn the hand-warmers the right way out and they are ready to wear.

MAKING THE HEADBAND

Knitting Step-by-Step

1. Cast on using the draw-thread method over the required number of needles in a one-by-one rib layout.
2. Knit the required number of rows in colour 1.
3. Swap to colour 2 and knit the same number of rows again. The last row is a loose row, and the carriage ends at the opposite side to where you want to start your cast-off.
4. Cast off using the loop-through-loop method.
5. Work in loose ends and finish the fabric.

Construction – refer to step-by-steps opposite

Now you have a lovely pair of hand-warmers and a headband... and if you made them to match the scarf from Chapter 2 you will have a full set of winter warmers! These small projects can also make great gifts; the hand-warmers can be made with any punch-card design, or you could just go for some stripes or a block colour – there are so many options.

1. To finish off your knitted headband, start by bring the ends together and fold them as pictured.

2. Sew the ends together in this position.

3. Bring the remaining fabric from each end together and cover the first seam.

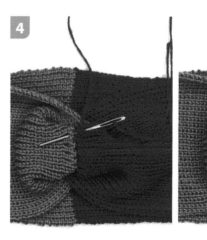

4. Sew these together. Tie off the yarn and turn the headband the right way out – it is now ready to wear!

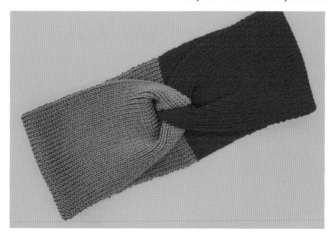

Completed headband.

CHAPTER 7

DESIGN YOUR OWN

In this chapter, we are going to look at designing your own knits, with a focus on garments. This chapter introduces neck and arm-hole shaping as well as trim details. These are just the basics; there are many more variations out there, but this section is designed to get you started.

At the end of the chapter, there is an example project. It is different to the other projects because it isn't made for you to follow along; instead, it is a step-by-step guide to the stages you need to go through for your own garment design project.

Shaping with one stitch transferred every knitted row.

SHAPING

Earlier in the book we looked at shaping and calculating frequency, using a shaped swatch as an example. Now we will look at how that frequency of shaping affects the resulting angle of the fabric and a few simple rules to help you remember how this works. The following samples have been created using different shaping methods and frequencies. You can see how transferring more frequently creates a gentler angle and the more rows you knit in between each decrease, the steeper the angle becomes.

In addition to a single stitch being transferred and taken out of working position, some garment shaping might require multiple stitches either to be transferred or cast off, depending on the required shape.

One stitch transferred every two knitted rows.

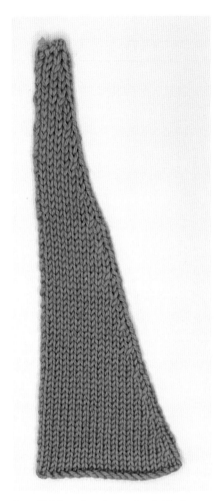

Two stitches transferred every two knitted rows.

Two stitches cast off every two knitted rows.

One stitch transferred every four knitted rows.

These techniques can all be used in garment shaping; which method/s you use will depend on the kind of shapes you want to create.

NECK STYLES

When designing your own garment, you are making all the design decisions; so, if you are designing a top, you will need to decide on the style of neckline you want. You might want a slash neck, or maybe a V; here I will go through how to knit a few commonly used necklines. At this point we are just looking at the neckline, but when you put this into a garment, you will also have armhole shaping to consider.

For now, follow the instructions to practise each neckline and familiarise yourself with the process. By doing this you will also have a sample of each one for reference when you come to designing your own garment. I have knitted all the swatches to include just the neckline area with a small border to avoid using up too much yarn. All the samples are knitted in four-ply sport merino yarn at stitch size 4.

We will look at how to apply this information to a neckline in the project at the end of this chapter.

Slash Neck

The slash neck is the simplest neckline as it doesn't involve any shaping – in fact, if you knitted the sweet and simple block jumper project in Chapter 3, you will have already created a slash neck. In that example, we added a trim to the neck, but slash neck (or straight necks) are often left without a trim.

A neat cast-off edge can work really well for a slash neck, especially if it is a simple top you are creating. You can just cast off both the front and back panels rather than taking them off on waste. This will reduce the elasticity of the neck slightly, so you need to make sure that the neck opening is big enough for you before linking the shoulder seams together.

Square Neck

To knit this neckline, first decide on the size of the neck open-ing – both the width and the depth – and either cast off the centre or remove it on waste, then knit up to the shoulder each side of the cast-off using partial knit. This kind of neckline is great for knitted vests.

You can do the exact same shaping on the back if you like, or, alternatively, you could create a shallower square neck by casting off the main section higher up the panel.

In the example shown here, the centre portion has been cast off; if you want to have open stitches so that a trim can be added more easily, you can simply take the centre portion off on waste instead. To practise knitting a square neck, follow the step-by-step instructions.

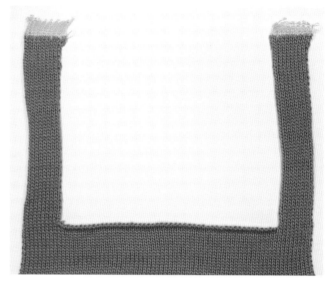

Square neckline knitted using partial knitting.

1. To knit a square neck, start by casting on over seventy needles and knit twenty rows.

2. Cast off fifty stitches in the centre for your neck opening.

3. Place the needles at the left-hand side in hold position and set the carriage to hold.

4. Knit the required number of rows for the vertical part of the neckline on the right-hand side – I knitted sixty. Remove this on waste.

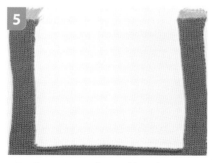

5. Set the carriage to knit and knit the same number of rows on the remaining needles, then remove this on waste as well.

This neckline can be really effective when working with a rib fabric, as it will lie flat much more easily than a single-bed fabric.

V-Neck

The V-neck is one of the simpler necks to figure out when it comes to calculating the shaping because you don't have the section at the start to consider – you go straight into shaping the V using decreasing, working one side at a time.

The first thing to think about, in addition to the neck opening width, is how deep you want the V-neck to be, as this will determine over how many rows you need to knit the neck area. For example, if you want a shallow V, you could knit it over fewer rows and would be decreasing more frequently, whereas a deeper V gives more rows to decrease over, decreasing less frequently and giving a different shape.

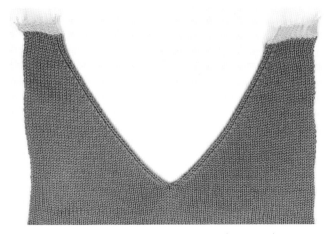

This V-neck sample was knitted over eighty rows, decreasing by sixty stitches, thirty on each side.

1. This V-neck sample is worked over eighty needles. To start, cast on eighty needles and knit twenty rows.

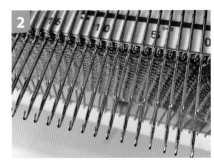

2. The first step is to split the V into two sections by pushing half of the needles up into hold position.

3. From here, knit one side of the V, decreasing by one stitch every two rows over sixty rows.

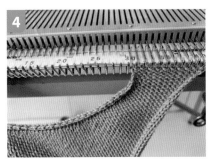

4. When you reach the top of this side, knit the last row as a loose row, then swap to waste yarn.

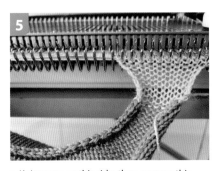

5. Knit waste on this side, then remove this half of the V on the waste yarn, and zero your row counter.

6. Set the carriage to knit, and knit one row over the remaining needles. Then close the small gap at the centre of the V by lifting the bump of the stitch at the edge of the right-hand side onto the first working needle in the left half of the neckline.

7. Knit the rest of this half of the neck using the same frequency, finish with a loose row, swap to waste yarn and remove this section on waste.

For the example in the photos, we are looking at a V-neck that on a garment would be around 15cm (6in) deep and is knitted over sixty rows making the neck opening around 18cm (7in) wide. To work out your own V-neck size and shaping, decide on the depth of the V and convert this to knitted rows; then the width of the neck opening and convert that to stitches.

When you have these values, divide the total number of stitches you will be decreasing by two before working out the frequency; this is because you will be decreasing on both sides of the V. Now use the frequency calculation to work out how many decreases are needed to reduce by your required number of stitches over the number of rows you are knitting the V-neck on each side.

Round Neck

The round neck is a classic, though it can seem a bit intimidating when you haven't done much shaping before. I put this one last as it combines the techniques you have used for the square and V-necks.

There are two options when creating a round neck: either casting off the central section and using stitch transfer shaping, or taking sections off on waste yarn and shaping. I would only use the first method if no trim was being added because it gives a less flexible base for the trim to be linked onto. The step-by-step photo sequence goes through the method of taking the central section off on waste; if you would rather cast off, simply cast off the same section that is taken off on waste in the example.

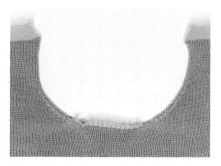

This neckline has been made by knitting the central section off on waste then shaping each side using transfer decreases.

1. This round neck sample is worked over seventy needles. To start, cast on seventy needles and knit twenty rows.

2. Take the central stitches off on waste yarn; I took off the central sixteen stitches for this neckline. First, push the needles at each side of this area into hold position.

3. Set the carriage to hold and knit waste yarn onto this section; I knitted ten rows here. You might need to add a weight to make sure it knits happily.

4. Press this area of knitting off by knitting over without any yarn, then take the first needle on the left into working position using the transfer tool so you don't lose the stitch.

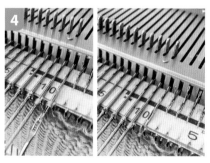

5. To avoid a stretched loop between the pressed-off area and the knitting area, lift the loop of the furthest left stitch on the pressed-off area onto the needle in working position. Set your row counter to zero.

continued on the following page

6. To knit the neckline, you need the needles on the left-hand side in working position. Simply push the needles back into upper working position, with the loops still behind the latches, and knit across.

7. Take the carriage back over so that two rows have been knitted. Using a transfer tool, decrease the knitting by two stitches, making sure you put the empty needles in non-working position.

8. You can use either a double- or triple-pronged tool to move the stitches by two places, or go for the fully fashioned decrease method here.

9. Knit two rows and decrease by two stitches four more times, until the row counter is at ten and you have decreased by ten stitches. After this decrease, we will be changing the shaping frequency.

10. Over the next eight rows, you will decrease by one stitch every two rows; again, you can just transfer the stitches or use the fashioning transfer method if you prefer.

11. The left-hand side shaping is complete. Now knit twenty rows just in this section, then either cast off or take these stitches off on waste.

12. With the right-hand set of needles still in hold position and the carriage set to hold, move the carriage over to the right of the knitting and retie the yarn to the leg of the machine.

13. Set the carriage to knit, and start the shaping by knitting two rows and decreasing by two edge stitches on the left of the neck.

14. Now follow steps 9 and 10 on the right-hand side over the following eighteen knitted rows. The shaping is now complete; knit twenty rows and remove on waste.

This example shows the depth and neck opening you will get by working over this number of needles. When calculating your own round neck, first find the width and depth of the neckline and convert this into stitches and rows. The easiest way to translate this into something you can knit is to sketch out the shape you would like over your desired number of stitches and rows on knitters' graph paper. From here, you can see how many needles you would want to take out in the centre, how many needles you need to decrease by and over how many rows you have to work.

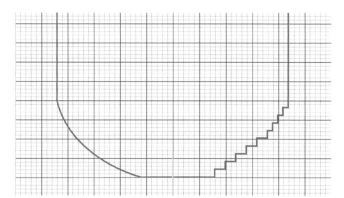

This is my shaping for a round neck opening, showing the curve on one side and this translated into stitches by following the graph paper on the other side.

GARMENT SHAPING

As we saw in the jumper project in Chapter 3, you can make a great garment without doing any shaping at all. Without shaping, however, you will always have a very straight fit with a boxy silhouette; to give you more options than that, we are now going to look at shaping in some other areas of a garment.

We have already seen how to shape the neckline in a garment, but that is just the beginning – by shaping the knitted pieces as you work, you can create any kind of fit you like. In these shaping examples I am going to use a standard long-sleeved, slightly cropped jumper as the basis to give a simple guide that you can adjust for your own needs.

Body Shaping

When designing a garment, you can choose exactly how much shaping to put into it, allowing it to fit your body exactly how you would like it to. If, for you, this means a straight body panel, then you can skip this bit. For me, it depends on the garment: one of my favourite short-sleeved knitted tops is completely straight in the body, but another is much narrower at the rib hem than at the chest. As with all shaping, you need to consider the kind of angle and shape you want to create, and think about how that translates into knitting. The diagram here shows a front panel labelled with stitches, rows and length measurements.

The shaping for the body on this example is minimal, with the number of stitches increasing from 132 to 166 over 104 rows. To get this shape I need to add thirty-four needles. Increasing on both sides of the panel means that I need to increase seventeen times over 104 rows. The frequency for this increase is six, meaning

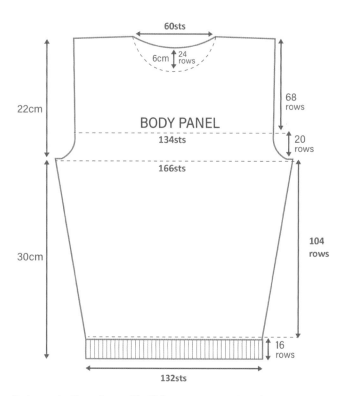

Body panel with sections, with stitches, measurements and rows per section to show where shaping will occur.

that to create this shaping I just need to increase on both sides every six rows.

For this part of the garment, the shaping is so straightforward it doesn't need to be practised; the most important thing to remember is to set the row counter to zero before you start so that you can keep track of where you are. Also, if the frequency isn't an easy number to multiply, for example increasing every seventh row, make a note of each row you need to increase on in case you lose count, or can't quite remember the relevant times table mid-knit.

Armhole Shaping

As well as shaping the sleeve (which we will get to soon), if you want the body of a garment to follow the shape of your underarm rather than just going straight up, you will need to put some shaping in here on the body panel too. How much you put here depends on how far you want the edge of the body panel to move in from the side seam, and it will match up with the shaping at the top of the sleeve.

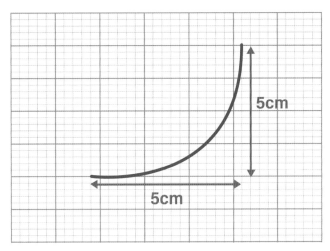

The sketched curve of the armhole shape labelled to show the width and height in centimetres.

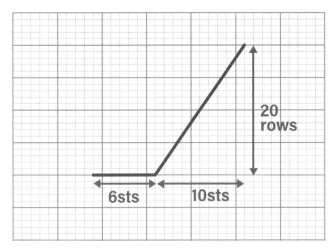

The armhole shaping transferred from a curve to an angular shape that more closely follows the squares on the paper, with labels indicating the stitches and rows being worked over.

This sleeveless garment by Lisa Land uses shaping at the top of the body panel for an interesting shape and fit.

You also need to think about how deep you want the shaped area of the armhole to be, as this will determine how many rows the shaping happens over. As you can see in the diagrams, I like to have a flat area at the beginning of the armhole, as I find it helps with the fit. This is the standard simple shaping that I like to put in on the body panel of a garment that is knitted in a four-ply yarn. Here, the armhole is coming in from the edge of the garment by 5cm (2in) over a knitted depth of 5cm (2in). The curve mapped out onto knitters' graph paper helped me to work out how many stitches and rows this would be worked over.

If you want to calculate your own, have a look at an existing garment and measure the armpit shaping. When you have this information, use the values from a tension swatch to work out over how many stitches and rows you will be working, and draw a curve out on knitters' graph paper as shown here. Sometimes you need to slightly adjust the number of stitches and rows over which the armhole is shaped depending on your tension – for example, working over fewer rows if it makes the decreasing pattern easier to work with, or adding a stitch to the area to make an even number.

The example in the diagrams is for a simple armhole that will have a sleeve attached to it, and when the underarm shaping is completed, the rest of the armhole is knitted straight. If you want to make a top without sleeves, you can use shaping here to narrow the body panel in towards the neck. This has been done on Lisa's garment (pictured) to create that shape.

Sleeve Shaping

When knitting sleeves, you usually begin with a cuff; we have covered both mock and true ribs in this book, and you can use either to start a sleeve. The kind of sleeve you are making and the trims you are using on the rest of the garment will affect your choice of sleeve cuff. I tend to use a true rib for anything long-sleeved and mock rib for short sleeves. This is a personal preference and you can use whichever trim you like; the true rib cuff will pull the sleeve in around the wrist, which is why it is so often used in long-sleeved jumpers.

If you knit a sleeve completely straight, due to the amount of fabric needed for the shoulder you will end up with a large opening for the hand and a loose-fitting sleeve. We are going to look at how to shape the sleeve to go from fitted cuff to underarm using increasing to widen the knitting area as the sleeve is knitted, and then move onto the sleeve head area. Earlier in the book we looked at shaping frequency; now we are going to apply that calculation to work out the sleeve shaping, starting with the area from cuff to underarm.

To work out your own sleeve shaping, you will need to know how wide the sleeve needs to be at the cuff and at the underarm points, as well as the full length of the sleeve and length from cuff to underarm. You will also need to have a tension swatch to give the tension measurement.

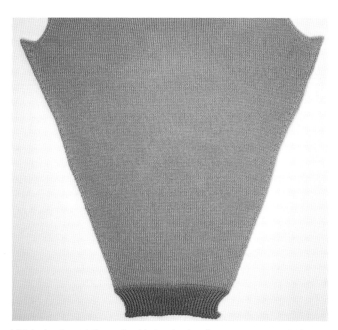

This is the shaped sleeve that I knitted using the measurements in the main text to create a sleeve that widens from cuff to underarm, with underarm shaping and a flat top.

For this exercise, you can either follow along with my measurements and knit the same size and shaped sleeve as me, or apply your own values to it. My tension for this sleeve was four rows per cm and 3.3 needles per cm with a cuff width of 20cm and an underarm of 44cm. This translates to sixty-six needles at the cuff and 146 needles at the underarm.

For the sleeve, I want a gradual increase over the whole piece, so I am going to work out the shaping frequency over the whole length from cuff to underarm. This length is 40cm, which translates to 160 knitted rows, and I will be adding two stitches at each increase point.

Current stitches = 66
Required stitches = 146
Difference = 80
The difference is the number of needles I will be adding.

Number of needles to add = 80
Number of increases = number of needles to add ÷ 2 = 40
Shaping frequency = number of knitted rows to increase over ÷ number of increases = 160 ÷ 40 = 4
Frequency = 4, which means we will increase every fourth row.

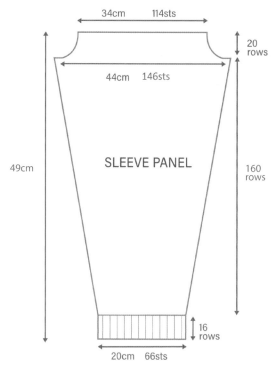

Plan for a shaped sleeve panel with all the measurements converted to rows and stitches; this will help with the calculations.

To knit this sleeve sample up to the underarm using my measurements, follow these steps:

1. Cast on sixty-six stitches, either using a one-by-one rib or a mock rib lifted hem, and knit the cuff.
2. Move to knitting the main sleeve, transferring to the main bed if needed, and set the row counter to zero.
3. Knit 160 rows, increasing one stitch at each edge every fourth row using the transfer increase method. This sleeve will be 146 stitches wide at the widest point.
4. Now for the sleeve head. We are going to shape this area to match with the underarm shaping on the body panel, and leave the top of the sleeve straight because this is the simplest way to work and still gives a good fit.
5. Set the row counter to zero, then use the exact same shaping as given in the example for the underarm. For this sleeve, I decreased by sixteen stitches over twenty rows following the same chart as for the underarm example on page 142.
6. You will start by casting off six stitches at each edge to create the flat part of this shaping. First, cast off the six stitches on the side closest to the carriage.
7. Now knit one row to take the yarn to the opposite side, then cast off six stitches at this edge of the sleeve panel.
8. Knit back over so that the row counter is at 2, and decrease by one stitch on both edges. Decrease again on both edges every two rows over the next eighteen rows; the row counter will read 20.
9. When the shaping has been worked on both sides, either cast off or remove the sleeve on waste.

Knitting a shaped sleeve is a great thing to try out before tackling your first garment because not only does it allow you to practise the shaping, it also gives you a sample that you can put against your body to see how it fits.

Shaped sleeve in progress on the machine using the transfer tool to widen the sleeve by two stitches every fourth row.

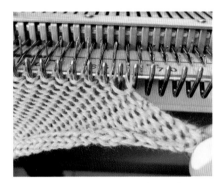

Stitches cast off at one edge to begin sleeve head shaping.

Sleeve head shaping continues, working to match the armhole using the transfer decrease method.

TRIMS

So far, we have looked at lifted hems and true ribs using the ribber bed, but there are more options when it comes to the welts and trims on your knits. Some of these more decorative trims were mentioned in Chapter 3, but here we will look at the subject in more detail. The following techniques give you a few additional options for more decorative trims; all of these effects can be applied to hems or necklines of garments.

Picot Edge

This simple technique transforms a lifted hem into a decorative trim, and all by just transferring some stitches: you are simply knitting a solid lifted hem with some lace hole transfers in the middle of it.

Follow these steps to create a picot edge hem:

1. Cast on and knit your solid lifted hem to the mid-point, where you knit the slightly looser row.
2. Use the transfer tool to move stitches, making holes in the fabric. I have moved every third stitch to create the picot edge, but it is up to you how many stitches you leave between your lace holes.
3. Leave the empty needles in working position so that they knit back on when you knit across.
4. Knit the rest of the hem, then lift the bottom stitches to complete the hem as you usually would.
5. Move onto knitting your main fabric.

You can experiment with leaving a different number of stitches between transfer holes to see what kind of effect it creates; this technique can also be combined with the next technique to bring a contrast edge to the trim.

Completed picot edge knitted using cotton yarn to get a crisp finish.

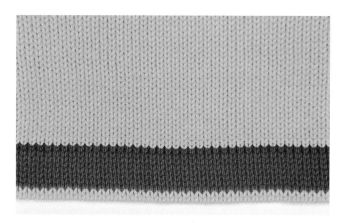

This whole trim was knitted over twenty-four rows, with rows 12 and 13 being knitted in a contrast colour to give this effect.

Contrast Tipped Trim

This technique is all about colour and adds a small stripe to the edge of your knitted trim. To achieve this, simply knit the middle two rows of your trim in a contrasting colour; when this is folded, the colour strip will sit on the very edge. If you want the edge stripe to be more obvious you can knit more rows, but the classic tipped trim is usually very thin, looking almost like the end of the knit has been dipped in a different colour.

A contrasting black and white trim has been knitted onto this colour-block jumper to add interest, and to reflect the inspiration for the design, which was Liquorice Allsorts.

First work a band of double crochet into the edge of the knit to provide a base for the decorative trim.

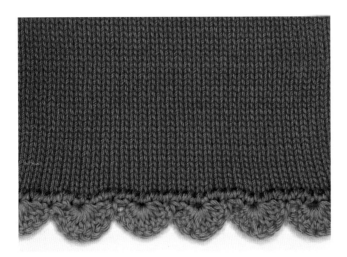

A scalloped pattern has been worked into the double crochet base to give a decorative trim.

Striped Trim

This is exactly what it sounds like, and can be a great way to add interest to a very simple garment design. Just decide on the stripe pattern that you want to create and knit it into the second half of the lifted hem; striping can also be used in rib hems to provide design interest in this area.

Crochet Trim

So far we have looked at machine-knitted trims, and how to knit and attach these, but there are other options. A crochet trim can give a decorative edge to any knit, particularly single-bed fabrics and garments such as knitted vests or shorts. These trims will not have the inherent stretch and recovery of a knitted trim but can give decorative effects that can't be achieved using knit.

To create a crochet trim, you simply need the right size of crochet hook and some suitable yarn; you can use the same yarn you knitted the garment with or a contrasting yarn – it's up to you. To check the hook size and yarn, I always test the trim out on my tension swatch before applying it to the garment, as you need to make sure the crochet doesn't distort the knitting. For the example illustrated here, the fabric was knitted using a four-ply soft cotton on stitch size 5, and I used a 2.5mm hook and four-ply cotton yarn for the trim.

I always work double crochet all the way around the edge that I am working into before doing anything fancy, which helps keep the fabric flat and even. When you have worked this foundation of crochet, you can add anything you like – a scalloped trim is one of my favourites. Small ruffles can be created by making a solid trim with increases, or, if you want something more delicate, open-work crochet can be worked into the double crochet base.

DESIGNING YOUR OWN KNITS

All the projects in this book provide a basis for you to develop your own designs, and I hope that you now feel confident to do that. By using the step-by-step instructions given, but with your own colour palette or a different knitted fabric design, you are creating your own designs! Doing this will help to build your confidence in designing and making anything from scarves to socks and simple garments. With this knowledge, you might well be ready to design your own knits from scratch. This process can be exciting and intimidating in equal parts. My best advice to make it feel more manageable is to design within your skill set – don't be too ambitious on your first go.

The idea for a knit can come from anywhere; for me it often comes from a swatch that I have knitted or a colour combination I would like to wear. When you have got your spark of inspiration, knit up some swatches. You will use whichever one you choose as a tension swatch anyway, so have fun and experiment. Don't forget to knit a trim on at the bottom of the swatches to test these out too.

If you are designing a garment, you will have an idea of the kind of shape you want – long or short sleeve, cropped or tunic length, and so on. If you are struggling to work out the shape, try sketching the idea out to get a feel for the design. One of the many great things about designing your own garments is that you are making them to fit you, and you can knit your garment pieces to the shape they need to be. Whenever I start with a shaped knitted garment, I use an existing garment to take measurements from; sometimes I use two different garments if, for example, I like the length of one but the fit on the chest of another. As well as measuring an existing garment, you might want to take your own measurements so that you can make sure whatever you are knitting will work for your body.

Armed with your tension swatch/es, sketch and measurements, you are ready to start planning your garment. Using the calculations that you have learnt through this book, sketch out each garment panel with measurements on it, then convert these to stitches and rows. Where you have shaping, use the frequency method to calculate how often to increase or decrease to create the desired shape. You will then be ready to knit and construct your garment.

The final project in this book is a 'design your own' example, showing you the process that I have gone through from initial idea to finished knitted garment. I hope you can use this guide and all the other skills you have learned from this book to design and make your own knits.

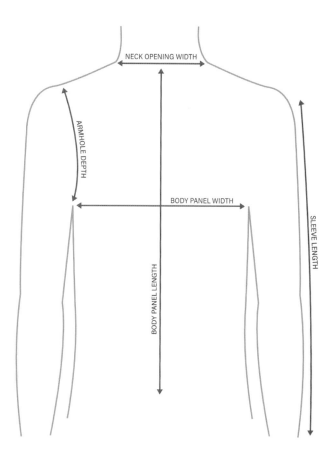

Where to measure on your body.

Shelby Marie Fuller for Elizabeth An'Marie

Shelby wearing one of her creations.

Punch-card fabric being knitted on Shelby's knitting machine.

My name is Shelby Fuller and I am the knitwear designer for Elizabeth An'Marie, located in Croydon, south London. I've been machine knitting for four years now. I love creating my own designs and characters to knit.

What brought you to machine knitting and where did you learn?

I started hand knitting as a hobby back in 2014. I enjoyed learning a new skill. One day I was researching different ways to knit and I came across knitting machines. Again, just as I taught myself to hand knit, I taught myself to machine knit.

Can you tell us about the knitting machines you use now and why they are the right machines for your practice?

I've been using the same machine I've had since late 2017, the Silver Reed SK280. This machine is amazing. At first, I would always knit the basics pattern, just the simple stockinet and rib stitch. But after learning and progressing I faced my fears to try punch card on the machine, and never looked back. The creativity is endless.

How about your design process – what inspires you?

Once I was someone who was very depressed, and I would wear black all the time, down to my shoes, even to the colour of my hair. But when I found knitting, I found joy again. The colours I once loved have now come back. Our famous smiley face was birthed out of that happiness. So I would say I'm inspired by colour, friendship and love – anything that could bring a smile to someone else's face.

When you've got your inspiration, how do you take it from idea to the finished product?

In 2021 I started writing down what I want to accomplish each month. My online shop opens every last Friday of the month. So, with each shop opening, I've already jotted down the theme/idea based on the season or what pattern or design I would like to launch.

Do you have any favourite yarns that you like to work with?

Merino. Merino all day!

Fabric swatches in Shelby's studio.

Garment in progress along with finished knits.

This chapter has been all about designing your own garment. Can you tell us about your process when designing a new garment?

First, I see what season I'm designing for (spring, summer or winter). I then pick my colours based on the season and decide if I would like to create a new punch-card design or use one of my past patterns. If not, I would create a new pattern or character (for our Smiley and Friends collection) and then we start to create. I love making vests. So much fun! And super quick to knit on the machine.

Do you have any useful tips for people designing and knitting their first garment?

Design something you know you'll love and want to wear every day. There's no point in making something you wouldn't want to show off to everyone.

Do you have any advice for people who are learning to use a knitting machine? Is there anything you wish you had known when you were starting out?

YouTube will be your best friend – there are so many videos of people using knitting machines now. Also, if you are someone who wants a face-to-face lesson, look up knitting machine shops or workshops near you. You might not believe it but there are so many out there. When I started, I wish I had just gone for the punch-card designs. It took me two to three years before I used one punch card. I was scared! But now I could never just stockinet stitch without a pattern involved.

Where can people find your work?

🌐 Elizabethanmarie.co.uk
📷 @shop_elizabethanmarie

Design your Own

Long-sleeved, shaped colour-block jumper with true rib cuffs and neck trim.

Yarns chosen for the jumper project; these were my starting point.

For this project, I will go through the process of designing and making a garment; to make your own, just follow the same steps but with your own design. To keep it easy, you can stick to the simple pattern panels provided in this project, customising with your own measurements and fabrics. This simple jumper can be translated and adapted in a number of ways depending on the shape, style and aesthetic you want to create. For example, a longer body with less shaping, or a shorter sleeve, will change the look completely.

STARTING POINT

Before you can knit anything, you need a starting point. This can come from anywhere – a colour palette, a yarn you want to use, a shape idea, anything. This will be different for everyone. My starting point for this garment was simply yarns; I have a selection of colours in four-ply merino wool that I have been using throughout the book and wanted to make a jumper with this quality of yarn. Rather than buying more yarn in any one or two specific colours, I decided to use what I already had and go for a colour block design using these.

GARMENT SHAPE

When you dream up the design, the shape is usually there with it. Especially if you are designing for yourself, you will have an idea of how you want the garment to fit and feel. For this project, I wanted a simple long-sleeved jumper with a slightly high ribbed neck and a slightly cropped length. These blank blocks can be used as a starting point for your own blocks. For example, you will see that the panels have some shaping, with the bottom of the jumper narrower than the chest; if you want a straight fit, just make the bottom width measurement the same as the chest.

For my garment, I will be using a true rib hem on the bottom of the jumper as well as on the cuffs. I want these to fit well to my wrists and body so am taking this into account when planning my body panels, with shaping in both the body and sleeves to achieve this fit. If you made the simple top earlier in the book, you will already have some measurements from that, although more will be needed if you want to adjust the shape.

In comparison to the rectangular top, the additional measurements that I took to make sure I had all the information for these garment panels were:

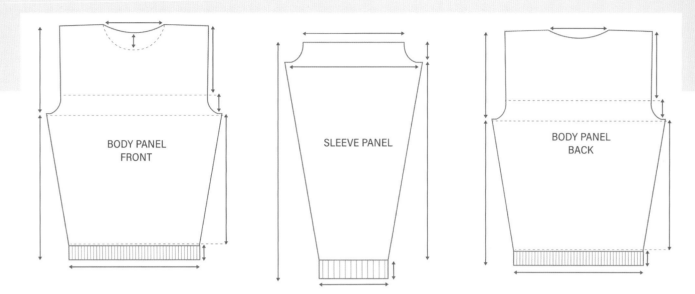

Blank shaped body, front, back and sleeve for you to add your own measurements.

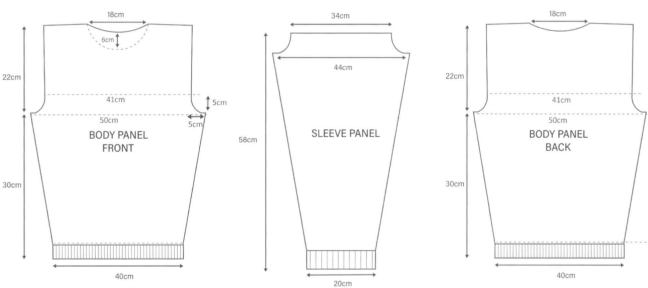

Shaped body, front, back and sleeve with my measurements.

Body panel width at rib

I used existing garments whose fit I like to get an idea of how wide I would like the bottom of the jumper to be for a snug fit.

Underarm shaping

Using an existing garment to work from, I measured the width and depth of the underarm shaping that I wanted for this area (see Armhole Shaping on page 141).

Neck depth

This is how far you want the neckline to come down at the front of the garment; again, I looked at a few existing garments to work out how deep I wanted the neckline to be.

Sleeve width at cuff

I measured around my wrist and checked the cuff area on existing garments to see how wide they are.

Single-bed plain knitting tension swatch with a rib trim.

TENSION SWATCHES

Once I decided on how big I wanted each garment panel to be, including the depth of the rib trims and the neckline, and had a rough idea of the body length, the next thing to do was knit the tension swatches. If you haven't used your project yarns before, you need to knit a swatch to work out the best stitch size for the yarns and knitting techniques. When you have worked out the desired stitch size and settings for the fabric/s, you can knit your tension swatch/es.

From this swatch, I then calculated my tension for the single-bed fabric. For the ribs, I used a previous project for reference and knitted sixteen rows based on this to get my 4cm (1.5in) rib trim. I would recommend knitting enough for the rib trim to allow you to measure it and find the rows per cm/inch. We will come back to the neck trim when we get there.

CALCULATIONS

Now you have the tension values for your fabric/s and the panels sketched out with measurements, simply convert each measurement from cm/inches to stitches or rows. Make sure you are using the right values for the right measurements: stitch values for all horizontal measurements and row values for all vertical ones. At this point, I sketch out the panels again and label them with the stitches and rows.

When you have done that, if you have shaping in the garment, that is the next thing you need to work out. I start with the body panel then move on to the sleeves.

Body Panel Shaping

Start by working out the shaping from the bottom of the garment to the underarm using the fashioning frequency calculations from Chapter 4.

Width at chest in stitches – width at bottom of garment in
    stitches = difference in stitches
Difference in stitches ÷ 2 = number of times to increase
Number of rows in section ÷ number of times to increase
    = frequency

Remember, if this doesn't come to a whole number, you can round it up or down, then check the number of rows this will come to and make any necessary adjustments. See Chapter 4, page 93 for more info on this.

Now looking at the underarm section, you will have a number of stitches and rows that you have decided to work over, so you just need to calculate what the shaping will look like for this. My underarm shaping is sixteen stitches decreased over twenty rows. Starting with a small flat section, I will cast off six stitches, then decrease by one stitch every two rows over twenty rows.

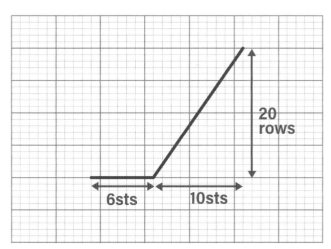

Underarm section labelled with decreases.

The next thing to consider will be the neckline shaping, which will vary depending on the shape you want to achieve. Use neck shaping samples to help you work this out. If you didn't knit any of those described earlier in the chapter, have a go at whichever shape you would like to work with. Using the information from these and your measurements for the width and depth of the neckline, you can work out the shaping for this area on knitter's graph paper.

For the back panel, you will follow the same shaping as the front panel up to the neckline, which will be much shallower on the back. For example, on the back of my garment, over fifty stitches, I cast off the central thirty stitches and shaped the ten stitches at either edge, decreasing by two stitches every two rows over ten rows.

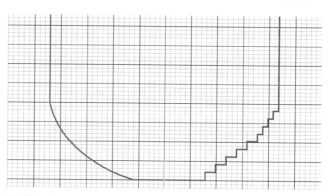

Neckline shaping on knitters' graph paper.

Sleeve Panel Shaping

The sleeve will be more straightforward than the body because the underarm shaping will be used on the sleeve head and this has already been calculated. You just need to work out the shaping from the cuff to the widest part of the sleeve, usually at the underarm.

Use the following calculations with your own values for stitches and rows to calculate the shaping frequency for the sleeves:

Width at underarm in stitches – width at bottom of sleeve in
    stitches = difference in stitches
Difference in stitches ÷ 2 = number of times to increase
Number of rows in section ÷ number of times to increase
    = frequency

Remember, if this comes to a number that isn't whole, you can round it up or down, then check the number of rows this will come to and make any necessary adjustments. With my sleeve panel, I knitted a straight section towards the top of the sleeve to accommodate the shaping over the rows that I had in the sleeve. Alternatively, you might lengthen the sleeve slightly to fit a few more increases in if this helps with the frequency calculation.

Sleeve panel labelled with stitches and rows.

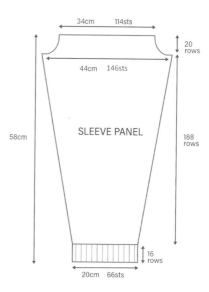

KNITTING THE PANELS

Now you have calculated all the shaping for the body and sleeve panels you are ready to knit them. As with all the projects, I make a knitting list for each of these; you can work from the sketches if you like, but I like everything written out step by step.

These are the steps that I write down for the following panels; simply insert your own values in the blanks:

Body Panels

1. Cast on over _____ needles in the required layout.
2. Knit _____ rows at stitch size _____ for rib.
3. Change to chosen yarns and technique for the main body panel, transferring to the main bed if necessary.
4. Knit _____ rows, increasing every _____ rows. Knit remaining straight rows to the underarm if needed.
5. Shape the underarm by casting off _____ stitches, then decreasing every _____ rows over _____ rows.
6. Knit _____ rows up to the neck shaping area.

Neck Shaping

Remember this will be different for front and back, so you will need to complete the chart twice.

1. Shape the neckline over _____ rows.
2. Take off _____ stitches in the centre on waste.
3. Decrease by _____ stitches over _____ rows in the following pattern _____.
4. Knit straight for _____ rows, with the last row on loose tension.
5. Knit waste to remove the shoulder area on waste yarn, then work the same shaping on the other side and remove this section on waste.

Sleeve Panels

1. Cast on over _____ needles in the required layout.
2. Knit _____ rows at stitch size _____ for rib.
3. Change to the chosen yarns and technique for the main sleeve panel, transferring to the main bed if necessary.
4. Knit _____ rows, increasing every _____ rows to the end of shaping, and knit to underarm.
5. Shape the underarm, casting off _____ stitches, then decreasing _____ stitches over _____ rows in the following pattern _____.
6. Knit the last row on loose tension, then knit waste to remove the sleeve on waste yarn.

When the panels have been knitted, finish these by washing or steaming, and block them to the required size for your project before starting the garment construction.

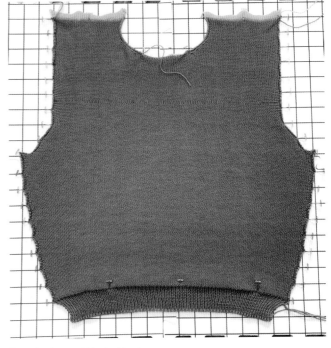

Front body panel blocked to size.

NECK TRIM

Now you have knitted all the panels, you can move on to the neck trim. As with the simple top, you need to join one shoulder seam before you do this (*see* the Chapter 3 project for a reminder on how to do this).

Depending on the neckline you chose, you might have all live stitches in the neck area, in which case you can simply count the stitches over which you will need to knit the neck trim. It is more likely that you will have a mixture of live and cast-off stitches; in this case, you want to hang the neck areas of both the front and back panels onto the machine to work out the size of your neck trim.

In the picture you can see that I haven't hung the live stitches back onto the needles; this is because I know exactly how many of them there are, so have just left a gap that number of needles wide on the machine. Also, note that the shoulder seam lines up with the zero on the needle bed.

When you have done this, make a note of the total number of needles; this is the size you will work to for the neck trim. You can work any kind of trim you like, usually matching with the trims you have knitted for the cuffs and hem.

For my jumper I have worked one-by-one rib trims in all other areas, so that is what I chose for the neck trim too. I have a total of 110 stitches over the neck opening, so my rib trim had to be knitted over this many needles, making sure I split these between the main and ribber beds in a one-by-one rib layout. Working in the same way as for the cuff and bottom rib trim, I cast on in waste and knitted a rib trim fourteen rows deep. The cast-on edge of the rib on the machine will be at the top of the neckline when worn, so it's important to make sure that it is neat and tight. When the trim is knitted, if rib is used, all stitches are then transferred to the main needle bed before attaching the trim to the body in the same way I did for the mock rib hem in the simple top project in Chapter 3.

When this is off the machine, press the neckline before joining the second shoulder seam. For this garment, I just linked the shoulder seam on the machine and joined the neck band by hand. This is because they are different colours, so I used pink on the machine to link the shoulder, then hand stitched the neck trim in blue.

Front and back panel necklines hung onto the machine.

Shoulder seam lined up with zero on machine and stitches hung onto empty needles.

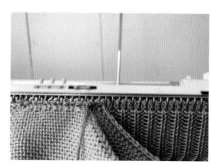

Ribbed neck trim on the machine with half the neckline hung onto it.

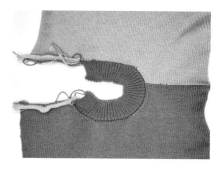

Jumper with neck trim added, pressed before second shoulder seam is joined.

CONSTRUCTION

You have linked the first shoulder seam and attached the neckline; now join the remainder of the garment in the following order, remembering to press each seam before moving on to the next one:

1. Second shoulder seam, including neck trim
2. Sleeves onto body panels – working from the underarm point all the way around, hanging the sleeve panel first, centring the middle of the shoulder over the zero on the machine, then matching the body panels onto this with the shoulder seam over the zero.
3. Side body and sleeve seam – work this all as one seam if you have enough needles on your machine; alternatively, if the panels are too long to both fit on the machine at the same time, work the side seam then the sleeve seam

Work in any loose ends, then block your garment to its required shape before wearing. And there you have it – your very own knitted garment, made by you, using your own measurements and design!

When you have completed your first garment, you can think about experimenting and making different shapes and even different garments. Through this book you have learned how to take measurements from existing pieces of clothing and apply them to your own designs, so there is nothing to stop you moving onto sleeveless tops, knitted dresses and skirts. Remember to consider the yarns you will be using and how much stretch and recovery these have, as well as shaping and trims to make sure your creations fit.

My jumper finished and ready to wear.

AFTERWORD

I hope you enjoyed discovering machine knitting with me, and that this book has helped you to become a more confident machine knitter. Even though it is full of techniques and processes, we have only just scratched the surface in terms of design potential for machine knitting. Each technique has endless possibilities, through the use of different yarns, colour combinations and application to different projects: I hope you enjoy exploring them all.

As well as experimenting with the skills you have learned through this book, there are many more to discover – from simple cables to tuck stitch punch cards, go and explore the wide world of machine knitting and see what else you can discover. When you find something you like the look of, see if you can apply it to one of the projects in this book, as long as you make that all-important tension swatch!

I hope that you will keep coming back to this book for reminders on techniques, inspiration, or just to make another pair of socks, but above of all, I hope that you have fallen deeply in love with machine knitting.

GLOSSARY

Carriage: This is the part of the machine with a handle on it; it works with the needles and yarn to form knitted stitches

Chunky gauge: A knitting machine that has fewer needles per inch than a standard gauge, allowing you to knit with thicker yarns and create chunky fabric

Clamps: Metal clamps that are used to attach the knitting machine to a table or suitable surface

Claw weights: Small plastic and metal weights with teeth that are hung directly onto the knitted fabric or onto a comb to apply tension to the fabric

Comb: A long, thin, metal comb with thin teeth that can be inserted into the fabric; it is used along with weights to add tension to the fabric when knitting

Decreasing: Removing needles/stitches from the knitting area

Domestic knitting machine: A knitting machine that has been made for use at home

Double bed: A knitting machine with two needle beds; also used to refer to fabrics knitted using two needle beds

Fair Isle: A style of knitting using two colours at a time; originating in hand knitting from Fair Isle, Scotland, in this book the term is used to refer to fabric created using punch cards

Fibre: The fine strands that are combined to make yarns; these come from a wide variety of sources and can be natural or man-made

Fine gauge: A knitting machine that has more needles per inch than a standard gauge, allowing you to knit with finer yarns creating thinner lighter fabrics

Finishing: The process of finishing your fabric after knitting so that it can be used - that is, working in ends, washing and blocking

Gate peg: The vertical metal pieces that sit between the machine needles; they help to keep the needles correctly spaced and aligned when they travel above the top edge of the needle bed

Gauge: The number of needles per inch on a knitting machine; the finer the gauge, the more needles per inch

Holding: Position in which the needles will hold onto the stitches and not knit them

Increasing: Adding needles/stitches to your knitting areas

Intarsia: A knitting process using as many colours as you like that creates a single layer of fabric with no floats on the back

Knocking off: Taking the knitting off the machine and leaving live loops at the top edge rather than casting off to create a closed edge

Latch needle: The type of needle that is in the knitting machine; it has a hook and latch that work together with yarn to form knitted stitches

Latch tool: Tool with an end that is the same as a latch needle

Lifted hem: A neat hem that can be created using one needle bed by lifting knitted stitches back onto the machine needles

Mast: The metal part of the machine that sits at the back of the needle bed and has the yarn feeder on it

Needle bed: The main part of the machine where all the needles sit

Needle butt: The part of the needle that sticks out of the needle bed when the needle is in its groove; this is the part that makes contact with the carriage to move the needle and in turn form stitches

Needle pusher: A small plastic rectangle used to push needles up into working position; it is flat on one edge and has gaps on the other to allow you to push every other needle up into working position

Partial knit: Also referred to as short-row knitting, this method uses holding to allow you to knit on just part of the fabric

Plating: Using two yarns together with a special plating feeder to align them so that one yarn is more visible on the ribber bed stitches and the other is more visible on the main bed stitches

Ply: This refers to how many strands of fibre have been put together to make the yarn you are using; two- and four-ply are common in machine knitting

Punch card: Card that allows you to knit patterns on a single-bed domestic knitting machine with a punch-card reader

Racking: The movement of one needle bed in relation to the other - the racking handle allows you to move the ribber bed in relation to the main needle bed

Ravel cord: A smooth, long cord that can be used to cast on with; it can also be used instead of waste yarn to create a division between waste and swatch/project knitting

Ribber: An additional needle bed that changes the machine from a single to a double bed and allows you to knit ribbed fabrics

Single bed: This refers to the main needle bed; single-layer fabric knitted on the main bed is often referred to as single-bed fabric

Sinker plate: The metal plate that screws onto the machine carriage; the yarns are threaded into here to knit

Slack: Term used to describe yarn when it does not have enough tension on it

Standard gauge: The most common gauge of domestic knitting machine

Tension: How tightly the yarn is being stretched, which is essential for the yarn to knit smoothly. Input tension is applied when threading by passing it through the tensioning discs and adjusting the setting to suit the yarn. Take-down tension is applied to the knitting by attaching weights to the fabric as it is being knitted.

Transfer tool: Tool with an eyelet at the end used to move stitches on the machine.

Tubular knit: Setting that knits a tube, knitting on the main and ribber bed on alternate rows.

Waste yarn: Yarn that is used at the beginning or end of a swatch or project and is removed after the swatch or project is completed.

INDEX

First published in 2023 by
The Crowood Press Ltd
Ramsbury, Marlborough
Wiltshire SN8 2HR

enquiries@crowood.com
www.crowood.com

This impression 2024

British Library Cataloguing-in-Publication Data
A catalogue record for this book is available from the British Library.

ISBN 978 0 7198 4199 6

Acknowledgements

There are so many people who have helped to make this book a
reality, from the ones who made things look good through photography and illustration to those who kept me supplied with tea
and snacks when I needed them. First up, a huge thank you to
Ben, who not only provided endless moral support and cups of
tea but also helped out in any way they could; I truly couldn't have
done it without them. Also, to everyone who has given me help
and advice along the way, or just listened to me go on about the
project – you're all the best!

The featured designers have brought such a great variety to
this book. It was really important for me to be able to showcase
the work of others, and without their time and effort I wouldn't
have been able to do that. Ria, Jonny, Gem, Jacques, Lisa, Marta
and Shelby: a huge thank you to all of you for letting me quiz you
about your practice and providing me with such great images to
show everyone the wonderful work you do, with additional photo
credit/thanks to Kayla Falcon (Marta's profile) and Felix Russel-Saw
(Ria's profile).

All of the illustrations you see in the book are by Jodie Allen,
whose style suits my work perfectly; it was really fun to work with
her. And then there's the photography by the super-talented and
lovely Lou White: getting the projects photographed by Lou was
a highlight of creating this book and I'm so pleased with how they
turned out. Additional photographs come from the wonderful
team at KNYT Nihan Azgurlu Dogru and Ibrahim Tekin, who
allowed me to showcase their fantastic intarsia.

Finally, I would like to acknowledge all the people who have
taught me to machine knit over the years, as well as all the people
who have shown me that you truly can machine knit anything!

Cover design by Sergey Tsvetkov
Typeset by Peggy & Co. Design
Printed and bound in India by Replika Press Pvt. Ltd.